PERSPECTIVES ON PEACEMAKING

Biblical Options in the Nuclear Age

**JOHN R. W. STOTT, WESLEY AND REBECCA PIPPERT
VERNON GROUNDS, MYRON AUGSBURGER, WILLIAM ARMSTRONG
JIM WALLIS, RONALD SIDER, MARK HATFIELD, DAVID BREESE**

edited by John A. Bernbaum

Regal
Books

A Division of GL Publications
Ventura, CA U.S.A.

Scripture quotations, unless otherwise indicated, are from the *Revised Standard Version* of the Bible, copyrighted 1946 and 1952 by the Division of Christian Education of the NCCC, U.S.A., and used by permission. Other versions quoted are:
NIV—New International Version, Holy Bible. Copyright © 1973 and 1978 by New York International Bible Society. Used by permission.
KJV—Authorized King James Version.

Published by Regal Books
A Division of GL Publications
Ventura, California 93006
Printed in U.S.A.

Library of Congress Cataloging in Publication Data
Main entry under title:

Perspectives on peacemaking.

Based on papers from a conference held in Pasadena, Calif., May 25-28, 1983.
Includes bibliographical references.
1. Peace—Religious aspects—Christianity—Congresses.
I. Bernbaum, John A., 1943-
BT736.4.P47   1984   261.8'73   84-3331
ISBN 0-8307-0951-7

Contents

95566

This book is dedicated to Chuck Shelton and Susan Baldauf, who faithfully pursued the vision which God had given them for a major conference of Evangelicals concerning peacemaking in the nuclear age and who selflessly worked to see it realized.

Acknowledgments

This book is a result of a labor of love on the part of many special brothers and sisters in Jesus Christ. Because it grew out of "The Church and Peacemaking in the Nuclear Age" conference, which took place in Pasadena, California, on May 25-28, 1983, the role of Chuck Shelton and Susan Baldauf and the conference's board of directors must first be acknowledged, for without their commitment and support the conference itself would never have occurred. Each of the contributors to this book also gave selflessly, and it was a privilege for me to work with people whom I so respect and admire for their leadership and for the powerful witness of their lives.

Dr. John R. Dellenback, president of the Christian College Coalition, is also to be thanked for his willingness to allow me to work on this book as an outgrowth of the Coa-

lition's ministry in education. Similarly, my colleagues
Jerry S. Herbert and Richard L. Gathro and our support
staff, John W. Hays and Kim Holt, assisted me in this
effort by assuming some of my responsibilities with the
American Studies Program in order to free me to work on
this manuscript; they were also a source of continual
encouragement. For both of these reasons I am thankful
for them. The Capitol Hill "Wednesday Lunch Group"
must also be recognized for their encouraging support and
their willingness to help me sharpen my thinking by serving as a sounding board for the ideas discussed in the final
chapter of this book.

Jo Anne Pierson played an important role in the preparation of this book as my primary typist, only briefly inter-
rupting her work in order to give birth to her second son.
Evelyn Jin also deserves to be recognized for volunteering
on several occasions to transcribe tapes of conference
speeches. Laurie Leslie Finlayson, my editor at Regal
Books, was also a joy to work with and her professional-
ism speaks well for the book's publisher.

Finally, my wife, Marge, was an indispensable assist-
ant in preparing this volume. She contributed hours of her
time to help in the editing of the chapters which follow and
to type various sections of the manuscript. She also supported me at home when I needed to go into hiding to
complete this book.

I feel a deep sense of thankfulness for all these people
and praise the Lord for their gifts of friendship, a friendship deepened by our common commitment to Jesus
Christ.

Preface

This book is the direct result of a significant historical event in modern evangelical history. In May, 1983, fourteen hundred people gathered in Pasadena, California, to examine the issues related to the nuclear arms race in light of the truths of Scripture. The origin and development of the plans for this conference deserve retelling because they are indeed a miraculous story.

The idea for a conference on biblical peacemaking was first formulated in the summer of 1979 by Chuck Shelton, then a Fuller Theological Seminary student. More than a year later, in November, 1980, he shared his idea with Susan Baldauf who was also a seminary student at Fuller.

In January of 1981, Chuck and Susan began to meet daily to pray about the possibility of a conference on this subject; by March, a group of peers joined them as prayer partners. That August, following their graduation from Fuller, they circulated a prospectus for a conference to eighty evangelical leaders; their overwhelmingly positive response affirmed Chuck's and Susan's sense of the timeliness of such a gathering.

Twenty representatives of prospective convening organizations met in January of 1982 in New York, Chicago, and Los Angeles to consider committing their organizations to such an event. On May 5, they reconvened in Pasadena to give firm shape to the vision. A board of directors was formed, representing a broad coalition of evangelical organizations, which assumed responsibility for supervising the conference staff and overseeing its financial solvency. The following organizations agreed to become conference convenors:

Bel Air Presbyterian Church
Calvin College
Christian College Coalition
Eternity Magazine
Evangelicals for Social Action
First United Methodist Church
Fuller Theological Seminary
La Cañada Presbyterian Church
Lake Avenue Congregational Church
National Association of Evangelicals
New Call to Peacemaking
Pasadena Covenant Church
Reformed Church in America
Sojourners Magazine
Voice of Calvary Ministries
Westmont College
Young Life International
Youth for Christ

In addition, another twenty-six evangelical organizations joined as conference affiliates and thereby contributed their energy and resources to supplement the efforts of the convenors.

At the board meeting on May 5, Chuck and Susan were formally given executive leadership responsibilities and, one month later, Jim Brenneman and Rebecca Jarrett joined as staff members. Beginning in September a thirty-member volunteer planning team began to meet monthly to coordinate the conference. Gradually, in ever-widening circles of support, God raised up people who offered their services to help facilitate the gathering which was eventually held on May 25-28, 1983. For anyone who watched this conference evolve, the only response could be, "Praise God" for how the evangelical community worked together like one body, with many diverse parts but united in purpose.

As the planning for the conference developed, the following questions provided a framework of inquiry:

1. *The Situation:* What is the present level of development of nuclear weaponry in the United States and the world?

2. *The Biblical Insights:* How should we understand the problem of nuclear weapons in the light of biblical teaching on war, peace, and human rights?

3. *Our Faithful Response:* How should we, as individual Christians and as the corporate Body of Christ, respond to the situation in light of the biblical insights?

Discussion concerning the answers to these questions was based on a set of affirmations agreed to by the board of directors:

• the Lordship of Jesus Christ and the authority of the Bible

• that biblical teaching reveals God's will for peace and justice

• that the biblical mandate calls the Body of Christ and individual Christians to serve as peacemakers

• that the ministry of peacemaking is understood differently by various Christian traditions

• that the respectful and earnest discussion of peacemaking among differing Christian traditions will edify the Church and,

• that such dialogue within the Church will equip Christians to respond obediently and effectively to the leading of the Holy Spirit.

The Pasadena conference was an important milestone in the development of evangelicalism because of its unique character. The gathering was unusual in the sense that the coalition of evangelical organizations which supported it included many groups with no previous history of cosponsoring conferences like this. While several of the organizations had an extensive record of administering their own conferences and retreats, few had engaged in such a common effort of cooperation.

Secondly, for many of the supporting organizations, sponsoring a conference on an issue as controversial as the nuclear arms race involved risks, including the possible loss of financial support. This was especially true for those groups whose mission was clearly in areas other than public policy. Despite the risks, these evangelical leaders were willing to put their organizations on the line out of a sense of obedience regardless of the costs.

A third unique dimension of the conference was the firm commitment by the board of directors and staff to base this gathering firmly on the Word of God. While other conferences and seminars have been held on the subject of the nuclear arms race, there was a singular commitment by the leadership to explicitly seek guidance from Scripture on this subject. This was reinforced by designing the program so that each day would begin with a Bible study and a time of worship and would end in similar fashion. Communal singing, which stressed themes of unity in the Body of Christ, and times of prayer and biblical reflection, which focused on the character of the Creator God, the Lordship of His Son, Jesus Christ, and the enabling power of the Holy Spirit, built an atmosphere of love and mutual respect.

This supportive environment contributed to the honest exchange of differing viewpoints which took place at Pasadena, an exchange which is again rare at conferences like this. Rather than choosing speakers who all shared slightly different versions of the same basic perspective or political persuasion, speakers with a wide range of positions on the nuclear arms race were chosen for this conference. They were asked to share their views on the issue of war and peace in the nuclear age as they have sought guidance from Scripture.

We have sought to preserve the unique characteristics of the Pasadena conference in this book. When the board of directors, following the conclusion of the conference on May 28, 1983, asked the Christian College Coalition to assume responsibility for conference follow-up, including the publication of a conference volume and other materials, we committed ourselves to producing a book for the Christian community which would honestly reflect the struggle of these respected evangelical leaders who sought to develop a position on the nuclear arms race in light of Scripture. In the spirit of the conference, several biblical passages and liturgies have been woven into the text to keep the reader focused on God's truth as it speaks to our time.

The Introduction by David Hubbard, who opened the Pasadena conference as the first plenary session speaker, sets the tone for this book. Hubbard openly shares his own difficulty in understanding these issues from a biblical perspective and challenges us to engage in honest dialogue with one another on the subject.

Part I, "Starting Point: Biblical Perspectives on Peacemaking," includes revised texts of three Bible studies which were given during the conference and material from a workshop led by Timothy Smith. These four chapters offer refreshing insights on the biblical view of peace and a Christian response to evil in the world.

Part II, "The Struggle of Christian Consciences," includes the revised texts of plenary session addresses by Ed Robb and Jim Wallis, expanded statements of panel presentations by Ron Sider, Richard Mouw, William Armstrong, and David Breese, and material from a workshop led by Myron Augsburger. The chapters by Vernon Grounds and Mark Hatfield are newly written especially for this book. While the content of Vernon Grounds's chapter was not presented at the conference, his presence in Pasadena was clearly felt by everyone who attended. He served as the master of ceremonies of the conference and his gracious, loving spirit set the mood for the three days of meetings. Mark Hatfield, who was unable to attend the conference because of scheduling conflicts, graciously agreed to share his own views by writing a chapter for this volume. Without his statement a volume on this subject would be incomplete in light of his leadership as a Christian in politics and as a respected national and international authority on the subject of peacemaking.

The final two sections are designed first to help the reader understand what these contributors share in common because of their commitment to the authority of Scripture and the Lordship of Christ and, second, to illustrate how the Bible is relevant to this issue of war and peace. Resources for further study are identified for the interested reader in Part IV.

Trying to understand what it means to be a peacemaker in the nuclear age as an act of obedience to Jesus Christ is not easy. There are no easy solutions to the complex issues that face us. The Apostle Paul, in his letter to the Philippians, shared these words:

> And this is my prayer: that your love may abound more and more in knowledge and depth of insight, so that you may be able to discern what is best and may be pure and blameless until the day of Christ, filled with the fruit of righteousness that comes through Jesus Christ—to the glory and praise of God (1:9-11, *NIV*).

It is our prayer that this book will help the reader to grow in knowledge and depth of insight into the issues relating to the nuclear arms race so all of us can discern what is "best" as an act of faithfulness to God and for His glory and praise.

John A. Bernbaum
Washington, D.C.
November, 1983

List of Contributors

WILLIAM L. ARMSTRONG was elected to the United States Senate in 1978 after serving three terms in the House of Representatives. He is a member of four Senate committees: Budget, Finance, Banking, and Government Operations. Senator and Mrs. Ellen Armstrong are parents of two children, Anne and Wil. They are members of Saint Matthew Lutheran Church in Aurora, Colorado, and attend Potomac Chapel in McLean, Virginia.

MYRON S. AUGSBURGER has served as an evangelist with Inter-Church Crusade, as president of Eastern Mennonite College and Seminary from 1965-1980, and is senior pastor of the Washington Community Fellowship in Washington, D.C. A graduate of Eastern Mennonite College and Seminary, and of Goshen Biblical Seminary, he holds the Th.D. from Union Theological Seminary, Richmond, Virginia. The author of fifteen books, he serves widely in evangelistic missions, and is often a Staley Lecturer on college campuses. His wife, Esther, is an accomplished artist. They have three children.

JOHN A. BERNBAUM is the director of the American Studies Program and Vice-President for Academic Affairs of the Christian College Coalition in Washington, D.C. Following his graduation from Calvin College, he completed his doctorate in European and Russian history at the University of Maryland. After four years at the Department of State as a historian-contributing editor of the *Foreign Relations of the United States* series, he began the American Studies Program in the fall of 1976. With his wife, Margery, they are raising a family of seven children. The Bernbaum family attends Fourth Presbyterian Church in Bethesda, Maryland, where John serves as an elder.

DAVID BREESE is president of Christian Destiny, Inc. of Wheaton, Illinois, a national organization committed to the advancement of Christianity through evangelistic crusades, literature distribution, university gatherings, and the use of radio and television. He graduated from Judson College and Northern Seminary and has taught philosophy, apologetics and church history. He has authored four books and regularly publishes a bulletin and a newsletter presenting a Christian view of current events. He and his wife Carol have two daughters, Lynn and Noelle.

VERNON C. GROUNDS is president emeritus of Conservative Baptist Seminary in Denver, Colorado. After serving as a pastor of the Gospel Tabernacle in Paterson, New Jersey for ten years, dean and professor of Theology at Baptist Bible Seminary in Johnson City, New

York for six years, he joined Conservative Baptist Seminary in 1951 as dean. He became president of that institution in 1956 where he served until 1979. He is a graduate of Rutgers University where he received his B.A.; his B.D. was granted by Faith Theological Seminary and his Ph.D. by Drew University. He and his wife, Ann, have a daughter Barbara.

MARK O. HATFIELD was first elected to the United States Senate in 1966 after two terms as the governor of Oregon. He previously served as state representative, state senator and secretary of state. After graduation from Willamette University in 1943 and Stanford University in 1948, with a bachelor's and master's degrees in Political Science, he taught at Willamette University. During World War II, he was a lieutenant J.G., commanding a landing craft at Iwo Jima and Okinawa, and served with the American forces in the China Civil War. Senator and Mrs. Antoinette Hatfield have four children, Elizabeth, Mark, Theresa, and Visko.

DAVID ALLAN HUBBARD is president and professor of Old Testament at Fuller Theological Seminary in Pasadena, California. Following the granting of his B.D. and Th.M. from Fuller Theological Seminary and his Ph.D. from St. Andrews University in Scotland, he taught biblical studies at Westmont College for six years before his appointment as president of Fuller in 1963. He is married and has one daughter.

RICHARD J. MOUW is professor of Philosophy at Calvin College in Grand Rapids, Michigan. He graduated from Houghton College in 1961 and received his M.A. from the University of Alberta in Canada and his Ph.D. from the University of Chicago. He has been teaching at

Calvin College since 1968. He and his wife, Phyllis, are raising one son.

EARL F. PALMER was educated at the University of California at Berkeley and Princeton Theological Seminary in Princeton, New Jersey. He is an ordained minister in the Presbyterian Church U.S.A. and has served in three churches: University Presbyterian Church in Seattle, Washington; Union Church in Manila (Philippines); and since 1970, First Presbyterian Church of Berkeley, California. He and his wife, Shirley, have three children: Anne, Jonathan and Elizabeth.

REBECCA MANLEY PIPPERT is Inter-Varsity Christian Fellowship's national consultant on evangelism, a position she has held since 1978. She received her B.A. and M.A. in English literature from the University of Illinois. She joined IVCF in 1972 as a staff member for private colleges in the Pacific Northwest and served in this position for five years. She is married to Wesley G. Pippert.

WESLEY G. PIPPERT is United Press International's manager for Israel, having previously worked for UPI since 1955 as a reporter assigned to the Congress and the White House. His work for UPI was interrupted for a year while he served as a press aide to Senator Charles Percy in 1967-68. He received his B.A. from the University of Iowa and his M.A. from Wheaton College. He is married to Rebecca Manley.

EDMUND W. ROBB, JR., is a ministerial member of the Northwest Texas Conference of the United Methodist Church. He served as a pastor for more than twenty years and has been an evangelist for fourteen years. He presently serves as executive secretary of the Ed Robb Evangelistic Association. In addition to these responsibilities, he serves as chairman of the executive committee of the Institute on Religion and Democracy. He is married and the father of five children.

RONALD J. SIDER is associate professor of Theology at Eastern Baptist Theological Seminary in Philadelphia, Pennsylvania. Following his graduation from Waterloo Lutheran University in 1962, he received his M.A., B.D., and Ph.D. from Yale University. From 1968 to 1978 he taught at Messiah College in Grantham, Pennsylvania; during these years he helped to found Evangelicals for Social Action and has served as its president since 1978. He and his wife, Arbutus, are raising three children; the Sider family attends the Brethren in Christ Church and Diamond Street Mennonite Church in Philadelphia.

TIMOTHY L. SMITH is professor of History and director of the Program in American Religious History at the Johns Hopkins University in Baltimore, Maryland, where he has taught since 1968. He is an ordained minister in the Church of the Nazarene and a graduate of the University of Virginia where he received his B.A. in 1943. He completed a master's degree and Ph.D. at Harvard University. Before joining the faculty at Johns Hopkins University he taught at Eastern Nazarene College, East Texas University, and the University of Minnesota. He is married to Anne Wright and together they have raised three children.

JOHN R.W. STOTT graduated from Cambridge University, was ordained to the ministry of the Church of England in 1945, and has served ever since at All Souls Church, Langham Place, London, first as curate, then for twenty-five years as rector, and from 1975 as rector emeritus. He has led university missions and spoken at students' and pastors' conferences on all six continents and has written twenty-five books. He is presently director of the London Institute for Contemporary Christianity.

JIM WALLIS is the founder of Sojourners Community in Washington, D.C., where he serves as a pastor. He is the editor of *Sojourners* Magazine, a preacher, an activist, and the author of several books. *Sojourners* is a magazine and a community committed to rebuilding the church at the local level, serving the poor, and peacemaking. He graduated from Michigan State University and attended Trinity Evangelical Divinity School in Deerfield, Illinois, where he and several other students founded the *Post-American*, which later became *Sojourners*.

Affirmation of Our Call and Task As Biblical Peacemakers: A Liturgy

LEADER	We come together confessing that Jesus Christ is our Lord, and He has called us to the tasks of peace and justice.
CONGREGATION	"For he is our peace, who has made us both one, and has broken down the dividing wall of hostility, by abolishing in his flesh the law of commandments and ordinances, that he might create in himself one new [person] in place of the two, so making peace, and might reconcile us both to God in one body through the cross, thereby bringing the hostility to an end" (Eph. 2:14-16).
LEADER	We affirm that wc have been called

to be peacemakers, to be called children of God.

CONGREGATION   "Let us then pursue what makes for peace and for mutual upbuilding" (Rom. 14:19).

LEADER   We acknowledge that our task must begin in our own reconciliation to God through Christ.

CONGREGATION   "Therefore, since we are justified by faith, we have peace with God through our Lord Jesus Christ" (Rom. 5:1).

LEADER   We confess that, as members of the Body of Christ, we are prone to let many things divide us, even as we seek to follow Christ together.

CONGREGATION   "There is neither Jew nor Greek, there is neither slave nor free, there is neither male nor female; for you are all one in Christ Jesus" (Gal. 3:28).

LEADER   Therefore, we confess our need to listen to one another with care, and to be open to the Holy Spirit.

CONGREGATION   "So if there is any encouragement in Christ, any incentive of love, any participation in the Spirit, any affection and sympathy, complete my joy by being of the same mind, having the same love, being in full accord and of one mind" (Phil. 2:1,2).

LEADER

We remember the biblical visions of the peaceful rule of God.

CONGREGATION

"He shall judge between many peoples, and shall decide for strong nations afar off; and they shall beat their swords into plowshares, and their spears into pruning hooks; nation shall not lift up sword against nation, neither shall they learn war any more; but they shall sit every man under his vine and under his fig tree, and none shall make them afraid; for the mouth of the Lord of hosts has spoken" (Mic. 4:3–4).

LEADER

But often times we are afraid of the task, of the dialogue, of each other, of the enemy. We confess those fears.

CONGREGATION

"Thou dost keep him in perfect peace, whose mind is stayed on thee, because he trusts in thee" (Isa. 26:3).

LEADER

The call of peacemaking is ours; it is a demanding one, which cannot be separated from the righteousness to which we have been called.

CONGREGATION   "Strive for peace with all . . . , and
                for the holiness without which no
                one will see the Lord. See to it that
                no one fail to obtain the grace of
                God; that no 'root of bitterness'
                spring up and cause trouble" (Heb.
                12:14,15).

LEADER   Despite the demands and scope of
                the task, we are absolutely certain
                of the resources of God which are
                ours in going out to do it.

CONGREGATION   "For you shall go out in joy, and be
                led forth in peace; the mountains
                and the hills before you shall break
                forth into singing, and all the trees
                of the field shall clap their hands"
                (Isa. 55:12).

LEADER   And we go together in the name of
                Jesus Christ, the Prince of Peace,
                through whom God reconciled all
                things whether on earth or in
                heaven, making peace by the blood
                of the cross.

CONGREGATION   "Now may the Lord of peace him-
                self give you peace at all times in all
                ways. The Lord be with you all" (2
                Thess. 3:16).

Introduction

Perspectives on Peace

by David Allan Hubbard

I need help understanding what Christian peacemaking in a nuclear age means.

I am struggling to see the issues whole and to see them clear. And I have eye trouble. Eye trouble of several kinds—enough eye trouble to fill the waiting room of a clinic; enough strange symptoms to crowd the ophthalmologist's chart.

A distinguished Christian leader once paused outside a restaurant to look at an American Cancer Society poster listing the seven deadly signs of cancer. I watched him sigh and then heard him say, "I've got every one of those."

I know how he felt. Almost every eye problem that one can have clouds, befuddles, distorts my perspective on peace and how we go about pursuing it.

Two things I want to share: First, my personal anguish

to gain perspective; second, a possible agenda to build consensus.

A PERSONAL ANGUISH TO GAIN PERSPECTIVE

Symptom One—Political Dyslexia: The strange switching of the letters of reality so that we cannot read situations with clarity and confidence.

The confusion of dyslexia is that we do not know if the letters themselves are wrong or our eyesight is transforming them.

Is the problem ours or someone else's?

I first faced my own political dyslexia after a brief stop in Viet Nam in January of 1968. Peaceful streets of Saigon, a normal Sunday morning service, a cheerful Chinese dinner at a pleasant restaurant, a quiet night at World Vision Headquarters across the street from the American Embassy. The only signs of war, an occasional uniform. The only sounds of war, a mortar shell exploding harmlessly beyond the horizon. Two weeks later the Tet offensive broke loose, and my whole reading of the situation was shattered. The waiters at the restaurant were among the revolutionaries. The gentle drivers of the rickshaws were Viet Cong. The interpretation I had received from our government was shown to be distorted beyond recognition by the Tet uprising. The major issue was not invasion but insurrection, not just enemies from the North, but rebels in the South. I was hurt, disillusioned, angry, ashamed. Was it my eyesight or the federal text that was mixed up?

I confess some of that same political dyslexia when I listen to the current statistics on the comparative strength of our armaments to Russia's.

I, for one, am at least willing to consider some approach to deterrence as a viable option, but I am thor-

oughly confused as to how to make a reasonable judgment.
Are the figures accurate? Are the comparisons fair? Is the
argument rigged? Am I being treated as a responsible person or manipulated as a political dupe? Can I trust our leaders? Or their political opponents?

Then comes the Bible, telling us how rulers should
rule:

> The psalmist's prayer: "Give the king thy justice,
> O God, and thy righteousness to the royal son"
> (Ps. 72:1).

> Jeremiah's word: "Do you think you are a king
> because you compete in cedar? Did not your
> father eat and drink and do justice and righteous-
> ness? Then it was well with him" (Jer. 22:15).

> Isaiah's promise: "Righteousness shall be the gir-
> dle of his waist, and faithfulness the girdle of his
> loins" (Isa. 11:5).

Then comes the Bible, telling us how rulers should
rule, and telling us how few rulers rule that way.

We deal with our political dyslexia by setting up integrity checks for the people who cook our policies and serve
up our information. Are righteousness and faithfulness
what hold our leaders together?

Odds are high, we have found out, that a good share of
the blame for our confusion lies not with our eyesight but
with their spelling.

*Symptom Two—Ethical Tunnel Vision: The walled-in
narrowness of seeing only our own point of view and won-
dering how anyone can see anything else.*

I had been raised in a patriotic family. The Spanish-American War had opened Puerto Rico to missions and evangelism. My father had gone there to preach and teach in 1906. He had given an invocation at a rally where Theodore Roosevelt, whose heroics in that war had rocketed him to celebrity, was speaking—undoubtedly about the glories of America's conquest in the Caribbean. World Wars I and II were read as utterly necessary—their victories divinely rendered. And to top it all, one of my direct ancestors, appropriately named Israel Hubbard, had run the tavern where the Massachusetts Minutemen met to plan the shot "heard 'round the world."

I was puzzled by my older brother's pacifism but chalked it up to excess spirituality, unacceptable other-worldliness, even mysticism. Such was my attitude through World War II and the Korean conflict, which was waged while I was in seminary. And this remained my attitude up to Viet Nam.

Then I made a mistake. I met John Howard Yoder and was introduced to the "politics of Jesus" years before the book was written.[1] From Yoder I learned the historic roots of pacifism, the strong theological case that can be made for it, its exegetical underpinnings.

All of this did not make a pacifist of me—but it did cause me to take another look at all that I had believed about Christians and war.

Then comes the Bible with its prophetic vision of peace that blacks out the pictures of Yahweh's wars in the earlier history and holds out the lure of a better way.

Then comes the Bible with its broadening perspective on the greedy motivations for war, the ugly savagery that war induces, the mixed results of war—all an implied call to peace.

Then comes the Bible with its direct commands to peace, to a new relationship with enemies, to a new love akin to the Father's that cares for the unjust as well as the just.

My tunnel vision is both exposed and expanded. I face my temptation to be like the child in Frank O'Connor's short story.

> The five-year old had prayed hard that his daddy would return safe from the war. The prayer was answered. But now he had to compete with his dad for his mother's listening ear and soft feather bed:
> "Mommy, do you think if I prayed hard God would send Daddy back to the war?"
> "No, dear. I don't think he would."
> "Why wouldn't he, Mommy?"
> "Because there isn't a war any longer, dear."
> "But, Mommy, couldn't God make another war, if He liked?"
> "He wouldn't like to, dear. It's not God who makes war, but bad people."
> "Oh," I said.
> I was disappointed about that. I began to think that God wasn't quite what He was cracked up to be.[2]

Symptom Three—Theological Double Vision: The dilemma of seeing the two historic positions of the church— the Just War and the pacifist approaches—simultaneously and arguing with oneself about which approach best captures the message of the Bible.

In my own experience tunnel vision has given way to double vision and Viet Nam aggravated the symptoms.

I agonized over the trend of our students to become pragmatic pacifists because the Viet Nam war became increasingly hard to justify. Besides, our nation has not yet developed a way to let its citizenry express their views on whether a war is just. Only the elected officials can do that—and we as individuals have to face the choice of fighting a war we do not believe in or standing in clear violation of the law. No provision for selective conscientious objection has yet been offered.

I shared our students' revulsion of the war, especially after the Tet offensive. Yet I ached at their historical and biblical naiveté. I suspected a cheap pacifism as keenly as I would a cheap discipleship.

Then comes the Bible, pushing me almost to the point of paradox: the right of the magistrate to bear the sword; yet those swords to be beaten into plowshares. One strand dealing with the present world broken by sin and vulnerable to the violent; the other strand tethered to the future when the knowledge of the Lord covers the earth as the waters cover the sea.

But the double vision becomes even more spotty when the wielders are super powers, the weaponry massive, and the potential results cosmically devastating. The boundary conditions classically stated by Augustine for a Just War become almost impossible to envisage let alone enforce; yet an all-out pacifism looks like a one-way ticket to totalitarian takeover.

Then comes the Bible again nudging us toward a concern for peace. Granted that some wars in some places at some times may justly be called just, averting war is still the better way, especially where the consequences are incalculable, the results are unpredictable, and the gains are immeasurable.

Symptom Four—Historical Myopia: A shortness of perspective in which we are lured to press our noses against the present and squint at what we falsely label 'the real world' and the 'present urgencies.'

The pragmatic crowds out the permanent. Survival of the way of life, continuation of the mission, threatened persecution of the church—these live and vital questions predominate.

A veteran Christian leader in Viet Nam put it plainly: "No doves among the missionaries."

Commencement in 1970 found us in the midst of conflict on the Fuller Seminary campus. One group of our students, rightly concerned about the expansion of the war into Cambodia, wanted to make some kind of statement about our government's policies in the service. Another group, largely missionaries, were rightly concerned about the survival of the churches in Southeast Asia and announced that they would walk out of the service if any public protest were ventured. Within our graduating class were embodied very different interpretations of what God wanted from us in response to history.

When we are consumed with the pragmatic questions, we behave like evangelical hippies. We remain fettered to the now, peering through nearsighted eyes at the present, blind to the other dimensions of holy history, worried about lack of fluency in a language that has neither past nor future tense.

Then comes the Bible, clutching us by the nape of the neck, and pulling us back far enough from the quandaries of the present so that we can gain the full sweep of its perspective: its picture of creation as the ideal—unsullied by sin; its picture of eschatology as the ultimate—all strife removed, all weapons laid down, all propensity to war erased.

A POSSIBLE AGENDA TO BUILD CONSENSUS

This dreary catalog of problems adds up to a kind of intellectual *iritis*— a massive irritation that makes me blink and squint and rub. It makes me long for what only a better understanding of the Scriptures and the mind of Christ revealed in them can give. I need a cosmic cortisone that will strike at the heart of the irritation, clear the spots, assuage the pain, and flood me with relief. Failing that, I am not sure I want to open my eyes very wide.

None of these symptoms, these painful hindrances to full perspective, may touch you at all. They are mine. I have shared them with you.

But it is possible—just possible—that the way the Bible comes to bring some light and relief to each symptom may have something to say to all of us.

Can we find from Scripture's affirmations the beginning of a consensus? The agenda that I offer is not at all the most that we can hope and pray for. But I think it ought to be the least—the lowest common denominator of Christian concern and biblical agreement.

Let me outline its main points with only brief comments.

Can we agree that:

The eschatological vision is the Divine norm?

There are no more wars of Yahweh in an Old Testament sense. The prophetic vision and the messianic mission have rendered them obsolete. With the prophets and especially with the Christ, the new possibility is opened—love that reaches even to our enemies.

Pannenberg's latest book on the Church quotes a poem by Friedrich von Logau during the Thirty Years War.

> If Christ's way to change the world
> had been to persecute and kill
> why then he would have crucified
> those Jews who sought to do him ill.[3]

The prelude to final judgment is described as war in Revelation 19. But it is God's war, not ours. We are under orders to grasp the truth of the world to come and put it to work wherever we can, in the power of the Spirit.

Our ability to honor this vision of peace as the true picture of how life should be lived is our testimony to God's sovereignty, our chief expression of trust in His promises. The eschatological vision is the divine norm—the picture of the life He demands and will provide.

Can we agree?

And can we agree that:

It is that vision for which we hope, pray, and work?

A vision so bright demands more than quiet acceptance, passive appreciation. It is a call as well as a promise.

Our response is to live out as much of the fullness of the life to come as we possibly can—and to do so in the most tangible, practical ways.

We act out the vision

without an arrogance that boasts in achievement,
without an anxiety that doubts the promise,
without a despair that thinks nothing can change,
without an aggressiveness that violates the peace
we claim to seek.

But we do act out the vision.

Can we agree?

And can we agree that:

All political responses to the need for peace are ambiguous?

They are ambiguous because governments themselves are stamped with ambiguity. They are both the powers ordained of God of Romans 13 and the beast that crawls out of the sea in Revelation 13. As Christians, then, we can never give absolute allegiance to any one political structure or pledge unqualified loyalty to any one set of political solutions.

Caution, reserve, and guardedness are the best political postures for Christians, as well as large doses of humility, though we know that some political solutions may be much better or much worse than others.

The eschatological vision is not implemented by political decisions, but by divine intervention. There can therefore be no final resolution of our quest for peace by political means.

The Bible encourages support of government and permits opposition to government. But it *commands* prayer for those who govern. Only God can and will make all things new. What we can do is work for better government, oppose poor government, and above all pray for those who govern. All political responses to the need for peace are ambiguous, though some may be obviously better than others.

Can we agree?

And can we agree that:

More than one Christian approach is possible in the quest for peace?

This seems to follow necessarily from the ambiguities of this present age and its governmental systems.

Is it Christian wisdom, is it biblical insight that makes our alignments on these issues so predictable?

With my puckish, distorted sense of humor, I thought

of this recently when I read Harold O.J. Brown's peace for strength article in *Moody Monthly*[4] and Reo Christenson's plea for pacifism in *The Christian Century*.[5] Where is it written that the publication venues for such articles cannot be reversed? Would heaven and earth really fall? Can more than one Christian approach be possible in the quest for peace?

Can we agree?

And can we agree that:

Charity and patience are necessary to foster Christian unity?

Economic and political issues sorely sawed our churches asunder in the Civil War. Theology played second fiddle to the harsher instruments of regionalism.

Ralph Kuyper, sage and scholar, has been heard to say that whenever economics and theology enter into contest, economics wins. The same thing, I fear, may be the case in the politics of peacemaking.

Where the concern—more even, the *passion*— for peace is present, can we not accept that at face value, and experience Christian fellowship even where the *means* of seeking peace may be subject to debate? Charity and patience are necessary to foster Christian unity.

Can we agree?

CONCLUSION

If your perspective has any of the problems that I recounted from my experience and if this agenda for consensus holds any healing promise, then we can make our way through and beyond this book like the biblical blind man who at first saw people like trees walking and then went on to clearer vision.

A memorable scene for me took place at the 1970 commencement service when we were in the throcs of the

Cambodian crisis. I had introduced Senator Mark Hatfield and had stepped aside to welcome him, when I was astounded to see a huge banner being unfolded in the front row of the balcony by two of our students. I have already mentioned the tensions in our community on that occasion. I froze in my tracks, alert for needed action as the whole sign was displayed. Its huge letters put me at ease: "Blessed are the peacemakers. We are with you, Mark."

In his book *Between a Rock and a Hard Place,*[6] Hatfield has pointed to that event as a turning point in his ministry as a politician.

The old beatitude did its work then and still does. Blessed are the peacemakers. They are the kind of people who bear the very character of God.

And we can add to the beatitude in the spirit of the gospel: Blessed are those who go about the tasks of peacemaking with a heart for the peace of Christ's people.

Notes
1. John Howard Yoder, *The Politics of Jesus* (Grand Rapids: Wm. B. Eerdmans Publishing Co., 1972).
2. Frank O'Connor, "My Oedipus Complex," *Great Short Stories of the World* (New York: Reader's Digest Association, Inc., 1972), p. 156.
3. Friedrich Von Logau, as quoted by W. Pannenberg, *The Church* (Philadelphia: Westminster Press, 1983).
4. Harold O.J. Brown, "Is Nuclear Freeze a National Folly?" *Moody Monthly,* June, 1983, pp. 8-11.
5. Reo M. Christenson, "Christians and Nuclear Aggression," *Christian Century,* May 25, 1983), pp. 522-526.
6. Mark O. Hatfield, *Between a Rock and a Hard Place* (Waco, TX: Word Books, 1976), pp. 23-25.

PART I

Starting Point— Biblical Perspectives on Peacemaking

Old Testament Lesson:
God is our refuge and strength,
    an ever present help in trouble.
Therefore we will not fear, though the
      earth give way and the mountains
      fall into the heart of the sea,
though its waters roar and foam
      and the mountains quake with their
      surging.
There is a river whose streams make
      glad the city of God, the holy
      place where the Most High dwells.
God is within her, she will not fall;
      God will help her at break of day.
Nations are in uproar, kingdoms fall;
      he lifts his voice, the earth melts.
The Lord Almighty is with us; the
      God of Jacob is our fortress.
Come and see the works of the Lord,
      the desolations he has brought on
      the earth.
He makes wars cease to the ends of the
      earth; he breaks the bow and shatters
      the spear, he burns the shields with
      fire.
"Be still, and know that I am God;
      I will be exalted among the nations,
      I will be exalted in the earth."
The Lord Almighty is with us;
      the God of Jacob is our fortress.
                    (Ps. 46, *NIV*)

New Testament Lesson:
Blessed are the poor in spirit,
    for theirs is the kingdom of heaven.
Blessed are those who mourn,
    for they will be comforted.
Blessed are the meek,
    for they will inherit the earth.
Blessed are those who hunger and
    thirst for righteousness,
    for they will be filled.
Blessed are the merciful,
    for they will be shown mercy.
Blessed are the pure in heart,
    for they will see God.
Blessed are the peacemakers,
    for they will be called sons of God.
                   (Matt. 5:3-9, *NIV)*

Chapter One

Christian Responses to Good and Evil:
A Study of Romans 12:9–13:10
by John R. W. Stott

Most of us know Paul's letter to the Romans as a mighty manifesto of the gospel. That is to say, we concentrate on its first eleven chapters. For here, with his unique blend of logic and eloquence, Paul argues that all humankind are speechless before God in their guilt; that acceptance with Him is possible only by His sheer grace, only because of the cross, and only by faith in Christ; that we can enjoy a new life through the Holy Spirit; that out of the sufferings of the present creation a new and glorious universe is to be born; and that meanwhile God is working out in history His plan to unite Jews and Gentiles in His new society.

And there we often stop. But Paul does not. He goes on to write that we have to respond to God's mercies revealed in the gospel, to offer our bodies to Him, and through our renewed minds to discern His will and be transformed by it. Moreover, as chapters 12 to 16 make clear, it is supremely in our *relationships* that our transformed life will be seen. They will be relationships of love.

So the passage we are to study begins and ends with love *(NIV):*

- 12:9, "Love must be sincere."
- 13:8,10, "Let no debt remain outstanding, except the continuing debt to love one another, for he who loves his fellow man has fulfilled the law . . . . Love does no harm to its neighbor. Therefore love is the fulfillment of the law."

Between these two great exhortations to love, however, and to some extent interwoven with them, Paul introduces another theme, namely the existence of good and evil in our world and what our Christian responses to both should be.

Four times in our passage good and evil are referred to in juxtaposition to one another *(NIV):*

- 12:9, "Hate what is evil; cling to what is good."
- 12:17, "Do not repay anyone evil for evil. Be careful to do what is right in the eyes of everybody."
- 12:21, "Do not be overcome by evil, but overcome evil with good."
- 13:3,4, "Rulers hold no terror for those who do right, but for those who do wrong . . . . For he [the one in authority] is God's servant to do you good . . . . He is God's servant, an agent of wrath to bring punishment on the wrongdoer."

Now God Himself is good, wholly and perfectly good. But ever since Adam and Eve disobeyed His command in the Garden of Eden, and ate the fruit of the forbidden tree, "the tree of the knowledge of good and evil," we human beings have had a "knowledge," a disastrous experimental knowledge of evil alongside good, which God never intended us to have (Gen. 2:17; 3:5). Indeed, the whole of human history is a reflection in the public arena of the conflict between good and evil which rages within each of us. Moreover, the history of redemption is the story of how God, who (as Jesus said in the Sermon on the Mount) "causes his sun to rise on the evil and the good" (Matt. 5:45), because He loves all men equally, is working through Christ to destroy evil and to make goodness triumph in the end.

But how does love relate to good and evil? What attitudes to them does the God of love intend us to develop? That is the theme of our text. Let us look more closely at the four verses I have quoted.

The hatred of evil

12:9: "Love must be sincere. Hate what is evil; cling to what is good" *(NIV)*. We cannot fail to be struck by the close connection in this verse between love and hatred. Normally we regard them as diametrically opposed to one another. They cannot coexist, we say. Love expels hatred, and hatred love. But the truth is not as simple as that. For Paul immediately follows his command to love with a second command to hate—not of course evildoers (whom he later tells us to love and serve) but evil itself. Whenever love is "sincere" then, literally "without hypocrisy," it is normally discerning. It never overlooks or condones evil. On the contrary it hates it. For love knows both the harm which evil always does to people, whether the perpetrators or the victims of it, and the blessing which goodness brings them. Therefore, if we love people, we must hate the evil which harms them and cling to the good which blesses them. Otherwise we cannot claim to love them. Sincere love is neither sentimental nor sloppy, but strong. Since the love of God is holy love, the love of the people of God must be holy also. Genuine love discriminates between good and evil; it hates evil and clings to what is good. And in the next verses (10-13) Paul develops some of the good things we are to cling to—brotherly affection, mutual honor, zealous service, joyful and patient hope, and generous hospitality.

The non-repayment of evil

12:14,17-19: "Bless those who persecute you; bless and do not curse . . . . Do not repay anyone evil for evil. Be careful to do what is right in the eyes of everybody. If it is possible, as far as it depends on you, live at peace with everyone. Do not take revenge, my friends.

It would be impossible to miss the echoes of the Sermon on the Mount contained in these verses.

Paul writes (v. 14): "Bless those who persecute you; bless and do not curse."

Jesus said (Luke 6:28): "Bless those who curse you, pray for those who mistreat you."

Paul writes (Rom. 12:17,19): "Do not repay evil for evil . . . . Do not take revenge."

Jesus said (Matt. 5:39): "Do not resist an evil person. If someone strikes you on the right cheek, turn to him the other also."

Paul writes (Rom. 12:20): "If your enemy is hungry, feed him."

Jesus said (Luke 6:27): "Love your enemies, do good to those who hate you."

The alternatives are plain and unequivocal. To curse is to wish people evil; to bless is to wish them good and to pray for it. Moreover, our wishes and prayers are to be expressed in deeds. If we are not to wish people evil by cursing them, neither are we to do them evil by taking revenge. If instead we are to wish them good by blessing them, then we are also to do them good by serving them. Love is always positive. It never seeks their harm; it always seeks their good. Paul gives a few examples in verses 15 and 16. Love is sensitive, identifying with people in their joys and sorrows, rejoicing with rejoicers and mourning with mourners. Love seeks harmony. And love is humble, gladly associating with people of all classes and cultures, never considering anybody as being "beneath us."

We come back to verse 17, "Do not repay anyone evil for evil," and to verse 19, "do not take revenge." All retaliation and revenge are forbidden to the people of God. Not only must we never attempt to get back at those who injure us, but we must repent of the very desire to do so. All animosity, spite and malice are incompatible with the spirit of Jesus. For "when they hurled their insults at him, he did not retaliate; when he suffered, he made no threats" (1 Pet. 2:23). Instead (Rom. 12:18), "If it is possible," that is, "as far as it depends on you, live at peace with everyone."

The conquest of evil

Paul now elaborates further his prohibition of revenge. It is not enough to forebear it; we must actively promote its opposite. Leaving the rest of verse 19 for the moment (about God's wrath and God's revenge), let us look at verses 20 and 21: "If your enemy is hungry, feed him; if he is thirsty, give him something to drink. In doing this, you will heap burning coals on his head. Do not be overcome by evil, but overcome evil with good."

In a word, vengeance is to be replaced by service. To take revenge on people is to inflict some injury on them; to serve them is to promote their welfare. Thus, if our enemy is hungry or thirsty, far from making his situation worse by starving him, we are to relieve it by giving him food and drink. In doing this, Paul adds, we "will heap burning coals on his head." The phrase is much misunderstood. To be sure, being showered with burning coals must describe an acute sensation of shame. But why do we want our enemy to feel ashamed? Not to serve him right by publicly humiliating him, for such a motive would be incompatible with the context. No, the reason we want him to feel ashamed is not in order to embarrass him but in order to reclaim him, not to put him down but to lift him up, that is, to bring him to a better mind. Only so, instead of being ourselves "overcome by evil," shall we "overcome evil with good."

This magnificent climax to Romans 12, which contains the third reference to good and evil, demands further thought. It is one thing to hate evil, to recognize it for what it is and to set ourselves resolutely against it, for this is an essential ingredient of genuine love; but it is negative. The second stage is to refuse to repay evil for evil. This is negative too, though at least it has the constructive result of not adding to the world's accumulation of evil. It is the third stage which is the really positive one. It is not only the determination not to let evil overcome us; it is the determination to overcome evil with good.

The tragedy of repaying evil with evil is that we thereby increase the world's tally of evil. We allow ourselves to be overcome by it, and so we spread it. This is what Martin Luther King, in that great sermon of his entitled "Love Your Enemies," written in a Georgia jail, called the "chain reaction of evil." "Hate multiplies hate," he said, "and violence multiplies violence in a descending spiral of destruction."

Of course we cannot always avoid being "overcome by evil" in the sense of being oppressed or crushed by evildoers. We can, however, avoid being overcome by it in the sense of being induced to retaliate and so increasing it. To refuse to repay evil is to refuse to multiply it, and so to halt the escalation. But how can we go further than this, so that evil is defeated and so *decreased?* Only by an increase of good, and sometimes by such a positive, loving, serving response to evildoers that they are themselves actually won over to goodness. As Alfred Plummer wrote, "to return evil for good is devilish; to return good for good (and evil for evil) is human; but to return good for evil is divine."

Here, so far, is the threefold attitude to good and evil which should characterize God's people. First, we are to hate what is evil and cling to what is good. Second, we are never to repay evil for evil, either in thought (cursing) or in deed (retaliating), but be careful to do what is right in the eyes of everybody. Third, we are to overcome evil with good. Hating evil, never repaying evil, overcoming evil: this should be the threefold stance of God's new society. It would set us apart from the world outside. For the world compromises with evil instead of hating it; takes revenge against evildoers instead of forgiving them, and is thus overcome by evil instead of overcoming it. If the society of Jesus were to be faithful to the standards He has set for us, it would be a significant witness to His transforming power.

But we cannot stop there. There is a fourth attitude to evil which Paul goes on to develop (though many omit it). It concerns the duty of the state, and must be called—

The punishment of evil

All careful readers of Romans have noticed the contrast between the end of chapter 12 and the beginning of chapter 13, and indeed the tension within Romans 12:19 itself:

- 12:19 "Do not take revenge, my friends, but leave room for God's wrath, for it is written: 'It is mine to avenge; I will repay,' says the Lord."
- 13:3,4 "The one in authority [i.e. the official of the

state] . . . is God's servant, an agent of wrath to bring punishment on the wrongdoer."

The same vocabulary is used in both places. The words "wrath" *(orgē)* and "revenge" or "punishment" *(ekdikēsis* or *ekdikos)* occur in both passages. In Romans 12:19 they are forbidden to Christian people. Not, however, because wrath against evil and the just punishment of evil are wrong in themselves, but because they are God's prerogative. "Leave room for God's wrath," writes Paul. Again, "It is mine to avenge; I will repay, says the Lord" (see 1 Pet. 2:23). How then do God's wrath and retribution fall on evildoers? In at least three ways. First, in the process of social degeneration (which Paul has described at the end of Romans 1) by which God "gives over" to uncontrolled depravity those who deliberately smother their knowledge of God and of goodness. It is thus that "the wrath of God is being revealed from heaven against all the godlessness and wickedness of men who suppress the truth by their wickedness" (Rom. 1:18). Secondly, the last day will be a day of judgment, for those who are stubbornly unrepentant are "storing up wrath" against themselves "for the day of God's wrath, when his righteous judgment will be revealed" (Rom. 2:5). But in chapter 13 Paul writes of a third way in which God's wrath and judgment fall on evildoers, namely through the judicial processes of the state.

"Everyone must submit himself to the governing authorities," he writes, "for there is no authority except that which God has established." Again, "the authorities that exist have been established by God" (v. 1). "Consequently, he who rebels against the authority is rebelling against what God has instituted" (v. 2). We are not to think of the function of the state in terms of "authority" only, however, but of "ministry" too. For "the one in authority" (a generic reference which could include any state official from policeman to judge) "is God's servant to do you good." Again, "He is God's servant, an agent of wrath to bring punishment on the wrongdoer" (v. 4). Yet again, the reason we are to pay taxes is that the authorities are "God's servants, who give their full time to governing" (v. 6).

I confess that I find it extremely impressive that Paul writes of both the "authority" and the "ministry" of the state; that three times he affirms the state's authority to be God's authority; and that three times he describes the ministers of the state as God's ministers. I do not think there is any way of wriggling out of this by interpreting the paragraph, for example, as a grudging acquiescence to the realities of power. No. Despite the defects of Roman government, which were well known to Paul, he declares that its authority and ministry belong to God, and he instructs his readers to be submissive. He sees the God-given role of the state in terms both of rewarding those who do good (in my view there ought to be more state recognition of public service and philanthropy) and of punishing evildoers. We are back, you see, with good and evil, and this time with the state's responsibility to promote the one and punish the other.

It is evident that Paul was thinking of the state in the ideal. He knew that a Roman procurator had condemned Jesus to death. He also knew from his own experience that Rome was capable of injustice, as when he was beaten without trial in Philippi, although he was a Roman citizen (Acts 16:37). Thus the state could misuse its authority and misdirect its ministry. We ourselves, who have the great benefit of a complete canon of Scripture, also know that the same state, which in Romans 13 is called God's servant, in Revelation 13 has become the devil's ally, because it persecutes the church. There is no possible justification in Romans 13 for oppressive or totalitarian rule. So the command to be submissive cannot be regarded as absolute. There may be times (as there were for Daniel and his friends in the Old Testament, and for Peter and John in the New) when our Christian duty is not to obey but to disobey the authorities. The God-ordained purpose of the power they have been given is to promote good and punish evil; what shall we do, then, when they use it rather to punish good and promote evil? We must resist. "Civil disobedience" is a biblical concept. The principle is clear: since the state's authority has been delegated to it by God, we are to submit to it right up to the point where obedience to the state would involve disobedience to God. At that point it is our Christian duty to disobey the state in order to obey God. As Peter and the other apostles said to the Sanhedrin: "We must obey God rather than men!" (Acts 5:29; see also 4:19).

We come now to the problem of war and to the state's participation in it. Our biblical passage may by legitimate extrapolation be said to speak to this situation also. We have seen that the state has authority from God to punish evildoers. Since some evildoers are aggressors who threaten its security from outside rather than inside, it seems that the state has God's authority to defend itself against such people also.

An important qualification has to be added, however. The state's authority to deal with evildoers implies the right to use whatever force is necessary to arrest them, to bring them to trial and, if convicted, to pass sentence on them and punish them. For authority means power. To concede that the state has authority, and then deny that it may use force, would be a contradiction in terms. Nevertheless, the state's legitimate use of force is strictly limited to the task for which it is given. It is what the police and the army in civilized countries call "minimum force." Policemen and soldiers have no right to arrest anybody they want to or to use unnecessary violence, let alone to shoot people indiscriminately. No. It is only "evildoers" whom the state has divine authority to punish. And evildoers are particular and identifiable people who have done wrong and need to be brought to justice. Police action is essentially discriminate action. The biblical writers express their horror at the "shedding of innocent blood."

The same principle must be applied to war, and it has been in Christian tradition. According to the Just-War theory, the force used must be controlled and discriminate, and a distinction must be made between combatants and non-combatants. Although in modern warfare a whole nation may be said to be involved (directly or indirectly) in the war effort, yet we would surely all agree that at least such people as hospital patients, little children and imbeciles should be guaranteed non-combatant immunity. No such immunity, however, could be guaranteed in a nuclear holocaust. Death by blast, by fire, by radiation and by the subsequent breakdown of services would engulf everybody. That is why some of the most important categories of the Just-War theory are simply inapplicable to the nuclear age.

All Christians ought then to say with confidence that the use of nuclear weapons, being instruments of indiscriminate destruction, would be totally immoral, a blasphemy against God and His creation, and biblically indefensible. One may still, out of Christian realism, be a multi-lateralist—though urging the taking of unilateral initiatives. But whatever *policy* of arms control and arms reduction one argues for, the *principle* seems to me absolutely clear. "ABC" weapons (Atomic, Biological and Chemical), that most gruesome of all alphabets, being all indiscriminate in their effects, cannot in any way be justified from Romans 13 or by the Just-War theory, nor can indiscriminate use of conventional weapons. All indiscriminate slaughter is an intolerable offense to the Christian conscience.

I have sought to draw your attention to Paul's references to good and evil in Romans 12:9–13:10. As members of God's new society, we are to hate evil and cling to goodness. We are never to repay evil for evil, since to repay evil is to be overcome by it. Instead, we are so to do good to those who do evil to us that we actually overcome evil with good.

This does not mean that evil is never to be punished, however, but only that it is God's prerogative to do so. And one way He does it is through the state's administration of justice. For the state is God's minister both to reward good and to punish evil. This authority may by extrapolation be extended to the state's self-defense against an external aggressor. But only if its use of force is carefully controlled. A biblically educated conscience must condemn all weapons of indiscriminate destruction.

This consecutive treatment of the passage, which moves from the hatred of evil through the non-repayment of evil and the overcoming of evil to the punishment of evil, still leaves us with a double problem of harmonization.

First, how can evil at one and the same time be both not repaid ("do not repay evil for evil") and repaid ("I will repay," says the Lord)? Paul's answer to this question concerns the agency through whom the "repayment" is made. As individual human beings, we have no right to stand in judgment of one another. For God is the judge. But one of the ways by which He judges evil is through the state's administration of justice. We must not take the law into our own hands.

Secondly, how can evil at one and the same time be both "overcome" (12:21) and "punished" (13:4)? This is a more difficult question and lies at the heart of the debate between pacifists and Just-War theorists. All Christians can see the two reconciled at the cross. For God overcomes our evil in justifying us only because He condemned it in Christ (Rom. 3:24-26; 8:1-4). He did not overcome evil by refusing to punish it, but rather by accepting the punishment Himself. At the cross human evil was both punished and overcome.

How then can these two be reconciled in our attitudes to evil today? Christians cannot come to terms with any attitude toward evil which either bypasses its punishment in order to overcome it, or punishes it without seeking to overcome it. Certainly the state as God's agent must witness to His justice by punishing evildoers as they deserve. But Christian people also have to witness to His mercy by renouncing all personal animosity and revenge, and by seeking to serve and so win offenders. Whenever offenders repent, either through the state's administration of justice, or through the forgiving mercy of the offended party, or through both, their evil is simultaneously punished and overcome.

It is considerably more difficult to imagine such a reconciliation in war when nations rather than individuals are involved. But at least we must struggle with the dilemma. Whenever an evil aggressor threatens the security of the state, Christians are likely to polarize. Just-War theorists concentrate on the need to resist and punish evil, and tend to forget the other biblical injunction to "overcome" it. Pacifists, on the other hand, concentrate on the need to overcome evil with good, and tend to forget that according to Scripture evil deserves to be punished. Can these two biblical emphases be reconciled? At least we should be able to agree with this: if a nation believes it is justified in going to war, in order to resist and punish evil, Christians will stress the need to look beyond the defeat and surrender of the national enemy to its repentance and rehabilitation. The punishment of evil is an essential part of God's moral government of the world. But retributive and reformative justice go hand in hand. The highest and noblest of all attitudes to evil is to seek to overcome it with good.

Chapter Two

The New Testament Concept of Peace

by Earl Palmer

The word *peacemaker* appears in the New Testament in Matthew 5 and is one of the nine blessings that Jesus Christ gives at the beginning of the Sermon on the Mount, which is our Lord's commentary on the law.

Blessed are the poor in spirit, for theirs is the kingdom of heaven. Blessed are those who mourn, for they shall be comforted. Blessed are the meek, for they shall inherit the earth. Blessed are those who hunger and thirst for righteousness, for they shall be satisfied. Blessed are the merciful, for they shall obtain mercy. Blessed are the pure in heart, for they shall see God. Blessed are the peacemakers, for they shall be called sons

of God. Blessed are those who are persecuted for
righteousness' sake, for theirs is the kingdom of
heaven (vv. 3-10).

And then in the final Beatitude, the final blessing, our
Lord ties these blessings to Himself directly. "Blessed are
you when men revile you and persecute you and utter all
kinds of evil against you falsely on my account. Rejoice and
be glad, for your reward is great in heaven, for so men
persecuted the prophets who were before you" (vv.
11–12).

"Blessed are the peacemakers." What does the word
peace mean? What does it mean to be a peacemaker? Jesus
Christ, our Lord, Himself helps us to understand the
meaning of that word in His Thursday night discourse. In
that great text from John 13 through 16, our Lord dia-
logues with His disciples, and in the midst of that dialogue
He promises them the gift of the Holy Spirit. John 14:25-
27 reads:

> These things I have spoken to you, while I am still
> with you. But the Counselor [literally, the one who
> comes alongside], the Holy Spirit, whom the
> Father will send in my name, he will teach you all
> things, and bring to our remembrance all that I
> have said to you. Peace I leave with you; my
> peace I give to you; not as the world gives do I
> give to you. Let not your hearts be troubled, nei-
> ther let them be afraid.

And then finally in the sixteenth chapter, at the very
close of that Thursday night discourse, after our Lord has
baffled His disciples with figures that they cannot fully

understand and then tells them plainly that He is about to leave them and go to His Father, the disciples in verses 29 and 30 say, "Now you are speaking plainly, not in any figure! Now we know that you know all things, and need none to question you; by this we believe that you came from God."

Jesus answered them, "Do you now believe? The hour is coming, indeed has come, when you will be scattered, every man to his home, and will leave me alone." Literally within minutes, perhaps an hour or so, in the Garden of Gethsemane, this prediction was fulfilled as the disciples scattered.

Then our Lord closes with these amazing words, "Yet I am not alone, for the Father is with me. I have said this to you, that in me" (now He repeats it again) "you may have peace. In the world you have tribulation" (literally "pressure" is the word or "turbulence"); "but be of good cheer, I have overcome the world."

What does this word *peace* mean? Certainly in these three texts where our Lord Himself uses the word, three things have become clear about the meaning of the word. First of all, peace has its origin in God. It has its origin in our Lord Himself. It is His gift that He gives. In fact, He calls it "my peace."

Secondly, peace is an experience of healing, or an experience that occurs in the midst of pressure, in the midst of tribulation. The word *peacemaker* implies that. The Apostle Paul's term is the word *reconciliation*. When Paul gives his own commentary on the word *peace* in Ephesians 2:14-18, he adds the word *reconcile* to explain this peacemaking part of the meaning of the word *peace*.

This is also true in the Old Testament *shalom*. In the 250 uses of shalom in the Old Testament, some 60 of them have to do with the resolution of crisis, or the sense of safety after crisis is resolved. There is this sense of reconciliation, or peacemaking, where in the midst of turbulence, in the midst of crisis, a healing has occurred.

And then third, peace has a result. It is something that happens not only from God, not only in the midst of crisis, but it also moves through us and has a result in our lives. Righteousness and justice are the result of peace. It is "My peace I give to you; not as the world gives do I give to you" (John 14:27).

Here you have that sense of peace as fulfillment. Two-thirds of the uses of shalom in the Old Testament carried this sense of health or wholeness or fulfillment. It is one of the predominant messianic terms that is used throughout the Old Testament in referring to the fulfillment of God's plan.

As Christians we need to put into focus the meaning of reconciliation, the task and the experience of reconciliation, of peacemaking, that second meaning of peace, the peace that occurs in the midst of crisis, in the midst of pressure or tribulation.

It seems to me there are two levels or stages that make up the journey of reconciliation. The first stage is what I am going to call the "experience of restraint," or the "experience of repentance." In other words, the first stage describes a clearing away of debris, of slowing down, so that the next, deeper level can be experienced.

When this first level of peacemaking, of reconciliation, occurs, we call it restraint. I really think that is what is meant in 2 Thessalonians 2, when the restrainer force is introduced in that great text by the Apostle Paul as a force that brings restraint and clears the debris to prepare the ground for the deeper resolution.

It is what our Lord Jesus does in John 8 when a group of people capture a woman caught in the act of adultery and throw her right at the feet of our Lord and then challenge Him by saying, "In the law Moses commanded us to stone such. What do you say about her?" (v. 5). John, in his own observation of this event, says that they were tempting Christ. And twice in that John 8:1-11 narrative John tells us that our Lord stoops over and writes in the sand.

Now John does not show the slightest interest in what He writes, but twice he observed that Jesus stoops over and writes in the sand. Helmut Thielicke calls this the intervention of the majestic silence of God. What is Jesus doing in that incident? He is slowing down the action. He is restraining the event. He is not bringing peace. He is not resolving the crisis that is in the hearts of those who are already tempting God by what they have done. They do not care about the preservation of the family. They do not care even about the crisis of adultery. They said they caught her in the act of adultery but they have not brought the man. And what does our Lord do? The first thing He does is to slow everything down. In effect, He restrains that event.

He does not resolve it. The resolution will come later. In fact the shadow of the cross is over that event. The resolution, the forgiveness that He is going to offer to this woman, will have to be won for that woman by our Lord Himself because He interposes His own life between her and the crowd. But what Jesus does do is to protect the crowd from doing more harm than they have already done. They have already tempted God, but they have not yet committed murder.

When Jesus writes in the sand He slows the event down, restrains it. He protects the crowd, and He protects the woman. Twice He does this and, finally, He makes the statement, "Let him who is without sin among you be the first to throw a stone at her" (v. 7). And we are told in John's text that from the eldest to the youngest they walked away. So finally our Lord is left alone with this woman, and He says to her, "Woman, where are they? Has no one condemned you?" (v. 10). She replies, "No one, Lord." He says, "Neither do I condemn you; go, and do not sin again" (v. 11).

That is an example of restraint. It is an example of the first level of reconciliation. It is *not* reconciliation. Neither is it the healing of the woman or the crowd, but it is restraint. It is not the solution but is the step before the solution. It is a boundary that has been set up to protect people from doing more harm than they have already done.

Restraint is the role a police officer plays when a brawl takes place in your neighborhood. Most brawls, unfortunately, are domestic brawls—maybe a man and wife are fighting it out and somebody in the apartment building finally calls the police. The police come and enter into the situation and restrain the two people. They restrain the crisis but they have not healed it.

This is also the role that a peacekeeping military force can play, such as has been played in the Middle East. We would be foolish to say that the kind of fragile restraint present in Lebanon is peace, because there are deep anxieties, anger and all kinds of resentment, some of them new and some of them old, that have got to be worked through. But an international armed military peacekeeping force only serves as a restrainer. It is not the resolution. It is an intervention that slows everything down. At least that is what it is supposed to be.

Now when we restrain ourselves we call it repentance. This is what the Bible means when it talks about turning around, repenting.

Take the brawl between the husband and wife. When he goes about his business that day he begins to feel, "Wow, what a short fuse I have. I'm always blasting people over the silliest things. I feel terrible about this and I want to work it through." Now when he begins to feel this, a restraint begins to build up inside him. We call this repentance, the recognition of harm and danger.

Repentance may be what happened in John's account when he says that from the eldest to the youngest they left. Jesus turned the focus of the crowd back upon themselves. When they began to recognize their guilt and the harm and danger that lie in the course of action they were involved in, then they used self-restraint. However, it is still not peace. The person who says, "You know I am a very proud person" may be showing self-recognition. It may not yet be repentance, but it could be, and it could be the beginning of a turning toward reconciliation.

But it is still not peace. Something more must happen. What is this restraint, whether outer restraint or inner restraint? I will give you a word that describes what I think it is. It is *time*. It is opportunity. When we self-restrain, we give ourselves time, a pause. It is a pause that offers an opportunity, and as such it is a sign of God's grace in that He grants us time to repent. In other words, the fact that God allows us to repent is one of the signs of God's grace.

More must still happen. In the parable of the Prodigal Son our Lord magnificently portrays this sign of grace. As the young man is restrained in a sense by the change of circumstance in the country when the poverty and the famine hit, he comes to himself—that is self-restraint, that is the beginning of repentance. And then he says, "I must go to my father." And he turns himself toward his father. He is still not healed; that still lies ahead. The relationship with the father must first be healed and, finally, also with the elder brother.

But now he has turned himself toward the father, toward the possibility of reconciliation. And what he has is time. That gift of repentance that God gives us is a part of the mystery of the gift of freedom, the freedom by which we sin and then the freedom by which we can repent: it is the gift of time.

I think one of the most remarkable articles I have read on this subject is in Aleksandr Solzhenitsyn's book *From Under the Rubble*. This book is a series of essays, which Solzhenitsyn edited, mainly written from the Soviet Union by anonymous authors or under pseudonyms. One of the essays, by Solzhenitsyn himself, is called "Repentance and Self-Limitation." He starts the essay with the following words: "The blessed Augustine once wrote, 'What is the state without justice. It is a band of robbers.'" Even now, fifteen centuries later, many people will readily recognize the force and accuracy of this judgment, an ethical judgment about a small group of people as applied by extension to the state. Then Solzhenitsyn develops this argument. He basically traces the biblical principle of repentance and then states that the biblical principle of repentance is a virtue for human beings to practice; what we must do is apply that principle to states and to nations.

Solzhenitsyn defines repentance as self-limitation. When that crowd in Jerusalem, from the eldest to the youngest, walked away from that potential stoning incident, Solzhenitsyn would call that repentance because they self-limited themselves. They denied themselves the right to do harm, and they turned away. They turned around.

Solzhenitsyn then comments: "After repentance, once we renounce the use of force, self-limitation comes into its own as the most natural principle to live by. Repentance creates the atmosphere for self-limitation." He continues: "Self-limitation on the part of individuals has often been observed and described and is well-known to all of us. But as far as I know, no state has ever carried through a deliberate policy of self-limitation or set itself such a task in a general form, though when it has done so at difficult moments, as in some particular sector such as in food rationing or fuel rationing, self-limitation has always paid off handsomely." He says that when states have self-limited themselves they have always benefited. Yet he says he has never seen a state self-limit itself as a general policy.

He goes on to explain why. "Every trade union and every corporation strives by all possible means to win the most advantageous position. Every firm aims at uninterrupted expansion. Every party wants to run its country. Medium-sized states want to become great ones. Great ones want to rule the world." And then he says, "We are always ready to limit others, and that's what politicians are always engaged in. But nowadays the man who suggests that a state or a party, without coercion and simply in answer to a moral call, should limit itself, invites ridicule."[1] Solzhenitsyn then calls upon his own country—by the way, he wrote this while he was still living in the Soviet Union—and upon the United States and the other nations of the world to self-limit. In other words, to take part in the first steps of reconciliation. The first step to reconciliation then is that slowing down, that self-limitation. And when we do it ourselves it is repentance. It is what grants us time.

Now we as Christians do not glorify this time or this opportunity, but we are grateful for it. We do not glorify the absence of conflict, because our word for peace, *shalom,* is a bigger word than that. It is a word that has its origin in God's character and it has its result in God's justice and God's righteousness.

In the reconciliation mandate which we have we do not glorify the absence of war. For instance, we are not pleased when we break up a conflict between a husband and wife before they injure one another. But as Christians we have an instinct to want to see the deeper resolution occur. We want to see the healing occur so that we do not glorify the time that is given to us by self-restraint and repentance. But we are grateful for it and we live and work for it. And the reason is that we want to be close to one another.

This is why Paul does not want the Christians to leave Rome or Corinth and go up into the hills to escape the city streets. Paul wants us to be in close. He wants us to see the whites of the enemy's eyes, to be close enough to relate to these people, because God has a message of hope. Christians have the peace of God, the good news to share with the world. That is why we as Christians, though we do not glorify the absence of war or the fact that there is this first level of restraint, should not describe this as peace, because it still lacks the resolution, the health of *shalom*.

We ought to be grateful for restraint and we should call it what it is. It is time that has been given to us to be close to another human being in order, by the grace of God, to see the deeper resolution occur. This is the chief moral flaw in blood revolution and bloody suppressions of insurrections, because after such runaway vengeance is all over and all is quiet on the western front, then people are dead who might have been reconciled. Then it is too late.

We, as Christians, have an instinct for restraint. We have a concern to see restraint occur, to see this first level of the peacemaking task take place because we have a concern for the deeper level, a deeper peace.

What is the peace that is at the deeper level? We now must return to our first principles. Jesus gave us the clue when He said, "My peace I give to you; not as the world gives do I give to you. Let not your hearts be troubled." The Lord Jesus Christ, who gave us the peacemaking mandate in Matthew 5, also gave us the peace to go with it. The peace that we have from Jesus Christ is the peace that restores the four-fold relationship that makes up a human being: (1) our relationship to God, (2) our relationship to ourselves, (3) our relationship to our neighbor, and (4) our relationship to the earth. This is the anthropology of the Ten Commandments. It is also the anthropology of the Apostle Paul in Romans 1. It is the way God has made us.

For us, war and the crisis of human sinfulness is the crisis that causes a break to occur in any of these four relationships. When my relationship with God is broken, then I do not know who I am and I tend, because man and woman are incurably religious, to find something else to worship. So I choose idols, and I destroy the earth in my choice of idols. Thus my relationship with the earth is distorted when my relationship with God is broken. When my relationship with myself is flawed, and I cannot see myself as beloved in God's sight, then how can I love my neighbor? Or if my relationship with my neighbor is chaotic and harmful, how can I come and worship God?

Notice that our Lord in the Sermon on the Mount brings all of these four relationships into focus. We have four basic relationships, and the peacemaking mandate that our Lord Jesus Christ has given to us is the mandate that yearns for the resolution of broken relationships—our relationship toward God, toward ourselves, toward our neighbor, and toward the earth.

The peace of Christ also has a righteous result. It is interesting to me that the word *shalom* is translated by three Greek words in the Septuagint. This, of course, helps us to understand the way the word *peace* then comes into the New Testament. When the Septuagint translators were trying to find Greek words from *Koine* Greek to render the 250 usages in the Old Testament of *shalom*, they chose three Greek words. The sort of garden variety word is *eirene*, the word that is the linguistic root for the word *peacemaker.* It is the common word for peace in the New Testament.

We find in the New Testament what this word means just as we find out what shalom means in the Old Testament—primarily by studying how it is used in the text. That is the main clue to meaning. *Eirene* is a bland Greek word. In Greek it means very little; its basic meaning is "harmony" or "absence of war." While it is used in the New Testament, you might say it is enriched by the fullness of the Old Testament word *shalom.*

The other two Greek words are very interesting. In many of the places where shalom appears in the Old Testament, the Septuagint translators used the word *telios,* which means "fulfilled." *Telios* shows the sense of fullness that is implied in the eschatological nature of shalom in the Old Testament, this moving toward a goal—toward God's righteousness, toward His fulfillment. Peace has a goal; it is going somewhere. It is not just the absence of war. That is why we should not call it peace when the man and wife are not fighting anymore. We are concerned about the resolution of their relationship, about how they feel about their relationship with God, with the earth, with each other, and with themselves. This is the Christian instinct we have from the gospel.

The third word I find the most intriguing of all. It is the word *soter,* which is the word from which we get all of the salvation vocabulary of the New Testament. I have often thought that the Apostle Paul, when he uses the word salvation, is using it primarily as his Greek word choice to express the fullness of what Old Testament shalom is all about. Shalom is the integration, the healing, the salvation of a human being, where a person is made whole, where all the parts are brought together, and reconciliation has occurred between God and myself and the earth and my neighbor: it is now that I have been saved. It is a process that happens because of the cross of Christ and because of His victory over death and His victory over sin.

It is interesting that in the great scene in Luke 19, when our Lord calls Zacchaeus down from the tree, He says, "I want to spend tonight in your house." Zacchaeus comes down and our Lord spends the night with him. The crowd murmurs, "He's gone in to be with a tax collector, sinner." And then in the very next line in Luke's account, Zacchaeus stands up and says, "Lord, the half of my goods I give to the poor; and if I have defrauded any one of anything, I restore it fourfold" (v. 8). Now *there* is repentance—a real turnaround. He has self-limited himself. And then comes this great line from our Lord. After Zacchaeus says that, the Lord says, "Today salvation has come to this house, since he also is a son of Abraham."

Jesus restores Zacchaeus's identity and then He gives him this marvelous word—salvation, peace, shalom has now come. And notice that it has its origin from God. It is the reconciliation of a human being in which all the fragments are brought together and he is made whole. It has justice. It has righteousness in it. That is peace.

We are called to be peacemakers. I think one of my favorite scenes in all the Chronicles of Narnia is the final scene in *The Lion, the Witch, and the Wardrobe*, when Susan and Lucy get to ride on Aslan's back, and to run all over Narnia. C.S. Lewis says it is better than riding on a horse because a horse makes so much noise with his hoofs. Can you imagine riding on one of the lions from Trafalgar Square, holding onto its golden mane? Since they have soft feet they do not make any sound at all. Aslan runs through Narnia and makes one huge leap over the whole wall of the castle, and inside the castle are all these poor Narnians who have been turned to stone by the Winter Witch. Aslan de-stones them, and makes them all alive again.

Lucy and Susan get a chance to ride on Aslan's back and to be peacemakers with him, and to bring life to where there was no life, and to bring hope where there was none. But before that can happen, before they can ride on Aslan's back, some other things had to happen. A traitor, Edmund, had to be healed. Lucy and Susan also had to be made aware of a deeper magic which was manifested when Aslan broke that great stone table and took the treachery of Edmund upon himself; he conquered the deep causes of war and became the peace himself.

We cannot be peacemakers until there is peace in our own hearts first. I cannot be a peacemaker, I cannot ride on Aslan's back until he has broken that great table and has won the peace for me. This is where peace begins in the New Testament. "Peace I leave with you; my peace I give to you." It is a peace that comes from Jesus Christ. It is right that before we can be peacemakers in the world, we ourselves have to be made right first, right with God, right with ourselves, right with our neighbors, and right with the earth.

Note
1. Aleksandr Solzhenitsyn, "Repentance and Self-Limitation," *From Under the Rubble* (Chicago: Regnery-Gateway, Inc., 1981).

Chapter Three

The Biblical Concept of Non-Retaliation

by Wesley Pippert and Rebecca Manley Pippert

Matthew 5:38-48 reads as follows:

You have heard that it was said, "An eye for an eye and a tooth for a tooth." But I say to you, Do not resist one who is evil. But if any one strikes you on the right cheek, turn to him the other also; and if any one would sue you and take your coat; let him have your cloak as well; and if any one forces you to go one mile, go with him two miles. Give to him who begs from you, and do not refuse him who would borrow from you. You have heard that it was said, "You shall love your neighbor and hate your enemy." But I say to you, Love your enemies and pray for those who persecute you, so that you may be sons of your Father who is in heaven; for he makes his sun rise on the evil and on the good, and sends rain on the just and on the unjust. For if you love those who love you, what reward have you? Do not even the tax collectors do the same? And if you salute only your brethren, what more are you doing than others? Do not even the Gentiles do the same? You, therefore, must be perfect, as your heavenly Father is perfect.

Part I—by Wesley Pippert

In May, 1983, I was sitting in the press gallery as the House of Representatives debated a $453 million appropriation so the Army could continue to build Pershing II missiles. Congressman Ron Dellums from California offered an amendment to strike all the funds, in part because the Army had disregarded a congressional directive by going ahead with a contract for production despite insufficient flight tests; but worse because, as Mr. Dellums put it, "The Pershing II could take the world in quantum fashion closer to the brink of nuclear war."

These Pershing II missiles would be parked in West Germany and could streak to the Soviet Union in six to eight minutes. It would take Soviet missiles twenty-five to thirty minutes to reach the United States, giving us a small measure of time to double-check the computers that would alert us of a forthcoming attack, and to make certain that the data actually was correct.

But with a mere six to eight minutes, the Soviets would have almost no time to double-check. What if they detected a Pershing missile headed their way, very quickly retaliated with their own SS-20s and then it turned out that their computers had made a mistake, that we had not fired a Pershing? The Pershing, Representative Dellums explained, deprives the Russians of cautious judgment.

While Congressman Dellums was speaking, the Speaker Pro Tem for the bill that day, Congressman Anthony C. Beilenson, had to gavel for order several times because other House members were chatting so loudly that they were being disruptive. In the minds of some reporters and House members, the Pershing II debate that day was not the most important point in the bill, which was an overall supplemental appropriations bill. The more important point in their minds was a controversial rider on whether to extend or restore the west front of the Capitol. And the Dellums amendment was so assured of defeat that a roll call vote was not even called for. It was defeated.

What does this have to do with the Bible passage from Matthew 5? We knew that the Bible has a lot to say about the issues of war and peace, about justice and mercy, about love and hate. The Sermon on the Mount is one example from the New Testament.

I want to deal here with some of the Old Testament passages that are background to this portion of Scripture, particularly as those passages relate to the nation. The second part of this essay will dig more deeply into the passage itself and draw some conclusions about the personal implications of the Sermon on the Mount.

Last year I had a very jarring experience. Three times I read the Old Testament historical books in parallel: that is, 1 and 2 Samuel, Kings, Chronicles and the matching prophets laid side-by-side. I did so with an objective. I wanted to take each king of Judah and of Israel, and particularly those who had done right in the eyes of the Lord, and see how they handled the issues of peace and justice. I discovered anew what Hendrick Kraemer talked about when he spoke of the radical realism of the Bible. God's people, the people of faith, often hated; they often were murderous; they often committed sexual sins; they often waged wars. The judges were involved in a repeating cycle of wars. David's reign was bloody and so were the reigns of his successors.

Solomon may have asked the Lord for wisdom and for discernment, but he still took slave labor. Jehoshaphat, we read, did that which was right in the eyes of the Lord, but that did not prevent him from enjoying the booty of war. In one part I was shocked to find that the prophet Elisha got so irritated when some small boys twitted him about being bald that he cursed them in the name of the Lord and some bears came out and tore them apart!

There is a time for war, and a time for peace, the Preacher in Ecclesiastes tells us. Jesus foretold that in our day there would be wars and rumors of wars. On the matter of a buildup of military strength for deterrent purposes, Jesus Himself said in Luke that when a strong man arms his palace his goods are at peace (Luke 11:21,22). This mixture of war and peace in Scripture is very complex and hard to understand.

The radical realism of the Scripture has a lesson: it reminds us of the luxury and perils of being a zealot, locked into one position. The reality is that Christians in decision-making positions in the marketplace generally do not have the luxury of being a zealot. For example, when Mark Hatfield and William Armstrong voted on the 1984 budget, they could not choose either between a massive arms buildup on the one hand or disarmament on the other. Their only choice was a narrow one: Was the increase in military spending for next year to be 7.5 percent or 6 percent, an increase that would involve roughly only $1 billion in a military budget of almost $190 billion. The Bible often speaks about men and women facing just such narrow, often very blurred choices, and few of them are Zealots.

There is a tremendous value in debating, clarifying and

defining the pure points of view; it very well may be that God may call you to be a prophet in espousing a precise position. But be sure that that really is what God is calling you to do. As important as defending a position is, we need to talk with one another and hear what others are thinking and saying.

Robert Davidson, who is the moderator of the United Presbyterian Church, told of speaking at a local church about the nuclear freeze. After the service was over, a retired Army colonel approached him and said that he opposed disarmament, that he felt that it was against the will of God, and furthermore, the Soviets could not be trusted. Davidson said he told him, "Well, if you hold that view, we're liable to end by blowing each other up." "That's right," snapped the colonel, "the sooner the better."

We need to return to God's Word. In the midst of this talk of war and bloodshed in the Old Testament, there is that theme, that thread, that foundation of peace that is inexplicably woven into the fabric of the Bible. After I finished reading the Old Testament historical books for the third time, I said to myself, "He truly is a God of peace." He is the Prince of Peace, Isaiah says. Jesus is our peace, Paul says. And He brought us peace through the cross.

Ultimately, after the debate is over, after the final vote is taken, that fact —that Jesus is our peace—should make our behavior as individuals, our behavior as a nation, different. Several years ago my wife and I were talking to an esteemed Christian leader. At that time I was covering the White House under the Carter administration. "Jimmy Carter's problem," this Christian leader thundered, "is that he doesn't treat the Russians the way they treat us. I'm not sure you can be a Christian president and deal effectively with the Russians," he said. And I replied, "Sir," and my voice kind of cracked because I hold this man in tremendous awe, "if what you say is true, that violates everything I understand about the nature of God. God is a God of peace. Jesus is our peace."

We can look back into the Old Testament and find more examples of this peace that overrides the wars and the bloodshed. Even when Jesus said, "You have heard that it was said, 'You shall love your neighbor and hate your enemy,'" He was not referring to Scripture. Nowhere in the Old Testament does it say that we are to hate our enemy. Jesus was talking about what some of the Scribes had said in erroneously inferring that if you love your neighbor it means that you must hate your enemy. The law of retaliation, of retribution, an eye for an eye and a tooth for a tooth was not to be understood as a command that the injured parties were to have the equivalent. Rather it was held up as a directive that the injured party could retaliate only up to a certain point and no further. The law of retaliation was a law of the maximum and not a law of the minimum.

David, as we look in the Old Testament, was a good example of God's emphasis on peace. He warred against the Philistines, the Syrians, Moabites, Edomites, and the people from Damascus. In the process he solidified the Israelite nation. He was loved and praised by God. Yet when David wanted to build the Temple, God refused his desire because He said David's reign had been too bloody. God hates bloodshed. God loves peace. The overall thrust of the Old Testament seems to be that the power of God was used more as a warning to others than as an actual exertion of force. In his heart, despite his wars, David loved peace too, for his psalms frequently refer to peace. "Seek peace, and pursue it," David said in Psalm 34:14. It is clear that God praised David, not for his peacefulness, but because he executed righteousness and justice to all people.

In the Old Testament, the concepts of mercy, justice, truth, power, and peace often are related. In many passages two or more of these terms are mentioned in the same verse or in the same chapter. It is as if one implies the others; that one cannot truly be a peacemaker unless one also has a passion for justice; that one cannot truly speak truth unless one speaks of justice and power in a caring way as well. The psalmist in one notable verse brings all these things together when he says, "Steadfast love and faithfulness will meet; righteousness and peace will kiss each other" (Ps. 85:10).

Biblical writers, in talking about these concepts, used the same words to apply not only to individual relationships but also to relationships among institutions and among nations. So these things not only have a personal effect but also an impact in the world at large.

A nation, no matter how many peacemakers are in it, cannot always avoid war. I think history will bear that out. But the Old Testament does teach that in times of hostility, the person of faith negotiates. For example, Moses sent messengers to King Sihon of Heshbon with words of peace. Jephthah the judge negotiated. Even in the rules of war, in Deuteronomy 20, the Israelites were told that if they approached a city to fight, they must come with terms of peace. Some blunt conclusions can be drawn about the imperative necessity of the United States sitting down with the Russians to discuss disarmament.

A few minutes after the debate on the Pershing II missile, which I mentioned earlier, I looked down and saw Ron Dellums on the Republican side sitting next to Jack Kemp, an adversary philosophically if I ever saw one. Their shoulders were touching; their heads came together at a point, and they were locked in conversation like two close friends. Despite their differences, they were willing to negotiate.

Finally, the Old Testament warriors prayed first. Before they went to battle they asked God about it. After Joshua's death the people asked the Lord, "Who shall fight Canaan?" David asked the Lord, "Shall I attack the Philistines? Shall I pursue the Amalekites?" Jehoshaphat asked the prophets, "Shall I go to battle against Ramoth-Gilead?"

If we reach the point where hostility appears certain, we had better be sure that we have prayed about it. On the second floor of the Capitol, just off the rotunda, there is a prayer room that was actually created by an act of Congress about a generation ago. I tried to go there daily when I worked on Capitol Hill. I did not pray that members of Congress would come to Christ, although I hope that they do. I did not pray the ambiguous prayer that they shall have wisdom. I did not pray that there would be a Christian presence there, whatever that means. But rather, I prayed that they would work to make this a just and merciful nation and that they would pursue peace. I prayed those things in terms of the specific legislation on the floor at that time.

What I have found in the Old Testament is actually very modest but, at the same time, it is very profound. How can it affect us? We must see the world and what we can do clearly and realistically. We must talk to those persons that we do not agree with and encourage our leaders to do the same thing. Let us pray for justice and righteousness. As Paul said, "Shod your feet with the equipment of the gospel of peace." (See Eph. 6:15.)

When Martin Luther King got his Nobel Prize in 1964, he said, "I believe that absolute truth and unconditional love will be the final word in ultimate reality." Absolute truth and unconditional love—that is what Matthew 5 is about.

That brings us to the portions of Matthew 5 where Jesus asks us to do more. We respond not with passive nonresistance, not with retaliation. But we are to respond positively with acts of mercy and kindness across the breadth of our human experience, whether an act of violation has been committed against us, whether a lawsuit has been initiated against us, whether we have been put into forced service, whether a beggar comes to us, or whatever. We do good to them that hate us. We bless them that curse us, and we pray for them that abuse us.

Part II—Becky Pippert

Jesus stands against the old things, the Hebrew law of retaliation. As the new authority, He invites us not to resist the evil person. He tells us that we are to respond differently. We are to love our neighbor and our enemy. We are to do positive good in the face of evil.

There is a problem here and I would like to address that problem. In looking at more global issues, we often find that the system itself does not give us a lot of options. We are not able to respond with the purity that we wish in our position. The difficulty in applying this passage to relationships is that the system will never keep us, will never prevent us from responding in purity. The system will never prevent us from loving our enemy, from not praying for those who persecute us. The only thing that will keep us from doing that is the battle within.

The difficulty with the sayings of old is that really it is very satisfying! The sayings of old are the only things that I can relate to, the only things that I can really identify with out of my own experience. On the other hand, the new things frustrate and go against the grain. They are so unnatural, and that is exactly the point.

That is why Jesus says, "I will give you a new commandment, and the new commandment is that you must love." Why did Jesus feel that it was necessary to command? Because He knew there was nothing in our limited human experience that would teach us anything about the kind of love that He was talking about. He had to command us to love because it does not come naturally. It is not something we would ever do out of the immediacy of our own experience.

Jesus begins by describing a very typical response to pain in the old sayings. The old way is to respond when we are wounded by being angry, feeling revenge or retaliation. And then He gives us His perspective on how to deal with being unfairly persecuted, being despitefully used, being hated; and Jesus says we are to love, to bless, to do good. It is very difficult for us to grasp the radical impossibility of these words of Jesus unless we have had an occasion to put His words into context. And that occasion would mean that we have had an enemy, that we have been despitefully used.

Have you ever really had an enemy? Have you ever experienced someone who has despitefully used you? What is your first response when that happens? I do not know about you, but my first response with enemies is that I want to do them in. I want them to experience the pain that they have caused me.

Not very long ago I was mugged, held up at gunpoint. The man put the gun to my head and told me that if I did not do what he told me to do he would kill me. He said the first thing he wanted me to do was to give him my watch. I am ashamed to confess this, but my first response was anger. I was scared, but I was more angry than I was frightened because I thought, Who does he think he is? Who does he think he is that he can get away with this? And I'm afraid I behaved with little intelligence because I resisted giving him the watch, which is rather dumb in light of a loaded gun. He said, "Give me the watch." And I said, "No." He said, "I said, 'give me the watch.'" I said, "I said, 'no.'" And he said, "Well, why not?" A fairly intelligent question in light of a loaded gun; and I said, "Because my husband gave me this watch. If he had wanted you to have it, he would have given it to you." The final conclusion? I gave him the watch.

However, that experience made me reflect upon precisely this verse, and I have to say with shame that my gut response was not the gospel's response. I was angry. I wanted retaliation. Jesus says here, if someone is doing something unfair, you not only give your coat, which referred in context to the long covering that went down to the ankles; you offer your cloak as well. The cloak was the heavier, more expensive garment that protected a person from rain or sun and was even used for bedding.

Suddenly Jesus' words did not sound sweet. They did not sound like something I would like to needlepoint and put in my kitchen. They were tough. They were exasperating. They were impossible. I do not know that we can understand what Jesus is really calling us to do unless we have had a context in which we tried to apply the words and saw how difficult they were. The intensity of such an experience sadly clarifies the difference between the natural human response and the divine response.

What happens when we hear the words of Jesus and really want to put them into practice? More than anything else, I think His words expose our poverty. His words expose the helplessness that we feel in seeking to put them into practice. We cannot do it. We do not have the resources to put them into practice, and if there is a solution to be found, the solution is going to have to come from the outside. It is going to have to come from help beyond what we can muster.

We must acknowledge that the difference between the old sayings and the new sayings is the dilemma of our poverty. And the difficulty with acknowledging our poverty as Americans is that we are mortified about being weak.

Jesus may say He is glorified in weakness, but He's not going to be glorified in our weakness if we can help it. We want Him to be glorified in our strength. When we see the toughness of His words, and we face our poverty, we are mortified and we are ashamed.

It is at this point that Jesus says, "No, don't be mortified, don't be ashamed. What a wonderful discovery you have made! You are poverty-stricken. Do you know how lucky you are to see that? Blessed are you who are poor in spirit."

The only angle we ever have to God is our bankruptcy. The only angle we ever have to our Saviour is our poverty. The strength comes from the realization of our brokenness, not by our insistence on control. But we do not come by poverty very easily. We do not want to acknowledge it.

I think there are two things that we do when we see the toughness of these words of Jesus and do not wish to admit our poverty. Either we minimize the radicalness of Jesus' commands, or we try to elevate ourselves by over-spiritualizing our response.

How do we minimize the radicalness of Jesus' commands? Jesus says, "Love your enemy." What do we really think He means by that? As I work with college students and listen to them, and as I work with churches and listen to their confession, I get the impression that we really think that Jesus means, "Well, when you love your enemy—somebody who is really out to do you in—what that means is that when you see them walking down the street, you walk on the other side. You don't punch them out. You do your best not to cause controversy or conflict."

Jesus says something far more outrageous. Jesus asks us to love that person that has despitefully used us, as we would love a lover, as we would love a child. We begin to hear Jesus whisper to us that there is no sacrifice a lover would ever make for his beloved that is too great that we should not also make for an enemy.

This is a radical call and it is uncompromising. When we realize that we cannot minimize Jesus' commands, then we try to elevate our own responses. We over-spiritualize. Rather than acknowledge the great gap between our response and Jesus' standards, we spiritualize our responses by saying, "Who me, struggle? Why I just seem to swing from one victory to the next. Me get angry? Never. I love everybody."

There is a problem here, and that is that Jesus rather bluntly assumes that we will be angry and we will have enemies. He tells us that we are to love our enemies, assuming that we have them. Why would He ask us to love something we do not have? He also assumes that we are angry and says the issue is how to deal with it. Jesus does not over-spiritualize. However, He does not tell us that we are to condemn, condone, or justify evil. The wonderful thing about loving our enemy is that we can say they are an enemy. We don't have to pretend that they are really sweet and then love them. We are able to say, "This is an enemy. This is an evil person." Jesus is very blunt about this. We are not to over-spiritualize our responses.

But do you know the irony today? The irony is that with our compulsive need to be needed, with our tremendous fear of rejection, with our neurotic emphasis on being positive no matter what, where our identity is increasingly found in how you respond to me rather than being a child of God, we have probably blocked out a lot of negative experiences. We have difficulty acknowledging enemies and acknowledging anything negative.

We find Jesus' words to pray for those who persecute us hard to relate to, not because the world has changed, but because we have compromised so much. We are not on a collision course with our culture at the points in which our culture is godless because we want to be liked. We want to be affirmed. Our identity is in the fact that you like me. If you want to be liked by all people, I am afraid that Jesus is not the man for you.

How do we get from the first saying to the second without minimizing the commands of Jesus and without spiritualizing our responses? How do we get from the old way to the new? First, we must not flee from the reality of our poverty.

Indeed, we must be grateful that we finally have seen it. And then we must die to it. We must put to death the old response. However, we do not remain in pain. We do not live at the point of our poverty alone, but we use this poverty to draw us into deeper dependence upon God. So first we move from the old to the new by acknowledging our poverty, then, secondly, we move from self-sufficiency to God-dependency. We move into a deeper place with God. Christ is my identity. I leave my rights with Him at the cross. My meaning comes from the fact that I am His child. My identity is no longer dependent upon your response, and so your curses cannot harm me. You cannot take away anything from me because I have them with Christ at the cross. I am free.

Someone said to me the other day, "Christianity is such a crutch." I said, "You better believe it, and we are all cripples." Until we come to that place of brokenness, unless we leave our self-sufficiency and become dependent upon God in a way that we have not known before, unless we pray for a renewal of the Spirit in our lives, it will be very difficult to follow these verses.

We see our poverty. We move from self-sufficiency to a deeper dependence upon God. And then, thirdly, we must walk in the newness of the Spirit and not of the flesh. We must never lose the vision that love is a greater force than evil. That love is the only force that can conquer evil and love conquers evil not by asking, "How has my enemy treated me lately," but by asking, "Have I treated my enemy the way Jesus has treated me?" We are called to a new way, a radical way.

I would like to conclude with a story that illustrates better than I could possibly outline what it means to be new, to not be old.

Wes and I have a friend who is a very godly man, and when I first met him I was so impressed with the power that he had. He was very quiet, very unassuming, but the more I got to know him, the more powerful I realized he was. And then he said to me, "Let me tell you a story."

Many years ago my wife came to me and said, "You know, I'm really tired of you. I haven't loved you for a very long time, and I want a divorce." I said, "You can't mean this. I love you. I adore you. I want this marriage to work." She said, "I'm sorry, but I don't love you. I want out." So we separated.

It was only at the time she left that I experienced what it really means to be impoverished, what it means to die. I had to die to what my friends thought. I had to die to my pride. I had to die to my anger. I had to die to my priorities—I had put my career ahead of my family. As I would go to the cross and I would die, Jesus would begin to give me new life, and He would say, "You are right to want to die to this but I am going to give you something in its place."

I began to learn what it means to pray, and I began to pray for my wife. I found that I began to love her in a way that I had never known. I would go to her apartment house, very late at night, and

I would circle her apartment house, and I would pray blessings on this woman who said she no longer loved me, and I would love her, and I would pray for her and I fasted for her. As I did this I began to experience more of my poverty and more of the newness that Christ promises. I began moving from the old saying to the new sayings.

This went on for quite a while. My Christian friends began to say, "Listen, why don't you just go ahead and get the divorce? You've pursued her; you've been faithful."

But I knew God's voice by now. I'd gotten to know Him so well, and as I went into prayer, I would say, "Lord, I've had it, I can't take it any more." God would say to me, "Would you really do to her what I would never do to you? Would you really break covenant when I would never break covenant with you?"

He led me into Hosea. Hosea's wife was a prostitute who left him. Her life was so degraded that at one point she was going to be sold like a piece of meat. Hosea went back and he bought his wife, and he said, "I want you to come home. You will come home."

That was God's message to me. And so I continued to circle her house and pray. If I could tell you the joy of learning how to die, I would, but I don't know how. Four years went by and she came to me and said, "You know, I really appreciate the fact that you've loved me. I can tell that you do. But I want out of this marriage and I'm getting a divorce." And she did so.

I went to God again and said, "I have done everything you've asked. I've loved her. I love her now. What do I do now?" God's response was clear: "Would you really ever do to her what I would never do to you? Do you think I would ever divorce you? Do you think I would ever leave you? You must behave in the way that I have behaved to you."

Christian leaders said, "Get married. Find somebody new. Dump her. Why do you hold on to this?" But I could not get away from the message of my Saviour.

So I continued to circle her house. I continued to pray. I continued to fast. I continued to love her for another five years; and if I could tell you what it has meant to me to walk in newness, I would, but I do not know how. My friends think I am foolish to spend nine years. The only one who does not seem to think I am foolish is God.

About eight months ago we received a card from his children. The card went like this: "Joe, Carol, and Ann [not their real names] invite you to share in the celebration of the reuniting in marriage of their parents. For it was said on this day, lo, this is our God. How we have waited for Him. Let us rejoice and be glad finally in this day of our salvation."

New Year's Day I met them as a married couple. I did not think I was going to like her very much. I was wrong. She's wonderful! How could you be anything else but wonderful if you have been prayed for when you have persecuted, if you have been loved when you have abused? How could you be anything but without wrinkle and spot and blemish when you have seen the kind of love this text talks about? She was wonderful. As they left, he said, "Nothing is ever lost in the Kingdom of God; not one tear is wasted; even evil is not wasted in the Kingdom of God."

That is a parable to show us how to get from the old saying to the new. We must be willing to die so that we can live. We must be willing to admit our poverty and to go from self-sufficiency to God-dependency.

Chapter Four

The Holy Spirit and Peace

by Timothy L. Smith

One of the major developments in modern biblical scholarship is called *canon criticism;* it has great significance for Evangelicals, even though those who pioneered in it and some of those who are still leaders of it are not Evangelicals. These biblical scholars start out on the assumption that it is worthwhile to study how Hellenistic Jews and Christians perceived in their wholeness the canons of the Old and New Testaments, and what both they and their successors thought were their larger continuities or themes. Canon criticism was thus a reaction against the manner in which for a hundred years or more scholars had approached the Bible, fragmenting its study and concentrating more and more upon particular writers or particular passages.

This renewed interest in viewing the Bible as a whole

has not yet produced an authoritative exposition of two important themes that bind all of Scripture together: peace, and the promise of the Holy Spirit. If relevance to the present concerns of humanity is a proper motivation for biblical studies—and I think it always is—these two themes merit being the first and not the last subjects to be explored. We should study them for the light Scripture sheds on humanity's drift toward self-extermination in the violence of atomic, biological, and chemical warfare.

Consider, then, what the various parts of the Bible say about the relationship of the Holy Spirit to the Kingdom of God, and to the holiness, *shalom,* and joy that Kingdom promises to make in real human life.

Isaiah 32, beginning with verse 14, reads:

> The fortress will be abandoned,
>   the noisy city deserted;
> citadel and watchtower will become a wasteland forever,
>   the delight of donkeys, a pasture for flocks,
> till the Spirit is poured upon us from on high,
>   and the desert becomes a fertile field,
>   and the fertile field seems like a forest.
> Justice will dwell in the desert
>   and righteousness live in the fertile field.
> The fruit of righteousness will be peace;
>   the effect of righteousness will be quietness
>   and confidence forever.
> My people will live in peaceful dwelling places,
>   in secure homes,
>   in undisturbed places of rest (32:14-18, *NIV*).

A parenthetical sentence near the close of Saint Paul's Epistle to the Romans echoes this Old Testament pas-

sage. In chapter 14, he turns to a relatively minor difference between Jews and Gentiles in the Christian community at Rome—eating meat offered to idols. Many of the
Jews would not touch it and urged the Gentiles not to,
seeking thus to impose on all Christians their ancient pre-
occupation with symbolic taboos about food. Paul was a
faithful but Hellenized Jew. He lived by all the rigors of the
Pharisaic law when he was among his own people, but
showed by his behavior and his witness that he thought
such observance was not necessary for Gentile Christians, nor even in all cases for himself when he was with
them. "The kingdom of God," he wrote then, "is not meat
and drink; but righteousness, and peace, and joy in the
Holy Ghost" (Rom. 14:17, *KJV*). This is a wonderful sum-
mary, not only of what I think the prophecy of Isaiah and
the Epistle to the Romans were about—righteousness,
reconciliation, wholeness, and joy—but also of a central
theme in all the prophets and in all of the New Testament
epistles.

Moreover, both passages point to the grand promise of
Jesus that believers who seek the Kingdom of God and His
righteousness will receive everything they need. If you
read through Jesus' words of farewell in John 14 and 15,
where He declared that the Father would send the Comforter to those who love Him and keep His commandments, you see the theme of righteousness, peace, and
joy, repeated in the same sequence. "My peace I give unto
you," He said. And twice, He declared, "These things I
have spoken to you, . . . that your joy may be full" (John
15:11; see also 16:24).

Many evangelical Christians, of whom I am one, think
that the words that Jesus spoke on the day of His resurrection are the hinge upon which biblical faith turns. They
reiterate exactly the same promise, that righteousness,
peace, and joy will flow from the outpouring of the Holy

Spirit on believers. As the Gospel of Luke records the story, ten of the eleven remaining apostles were gathered behind closed doors on the evening of Easter day. They were sharing both their doubts and their dawning hopes that what some of the women claimed to have heard, and what first Mary and then Simon Peter claimed to have witnessed, might indeed be true. As they talked, Jesus stood in the midst of them and said simply, "Shalom," "peace" (Luke 24:36). This was not simply an old Jewish greeting; it opened for them life's most sacred moment. After showing them His wounds, the Lord breathed on them (the word in the original means the same as our word *inspired;* the Hebrew word for *spirit* is "breath") and said, "Receive the Holy Spirit" (John 20:21,22). In that moment He breathed the life of God into their lives so they would never need to doubt the presence of Him whose name is Emmanuel, the Prince of *Shalom.*

Then Jesus opened their minds, Luke's account tells us, so that they could understand the Scriptures, and He explained all that was written about Himself in the Law of Moses, the Prophets, and the Psalms. He taught them that night the meaning of the new covenant. From their childhood, they had heard of that covenant in the words of Ezekiel. To their generation, however, Judas Maccabaeus, who had led a revolt against Greek conquerors two centuries earlier, was still remembered as a hero. They had grown up hearing long debates over whether the Maccabean way of rebellion against foreign rulers was God's plan for inaugurating the new covenant. They had become followers of John the Baptist and then of Jesus, knowing that both rejected the call of the Zealots for a rebellion against Rome, and that neither believed that a revival of Jewish nationalism was necessary to prepare the way for Messiah's kingdom. Jesus and John had taught them that the hope of the new covenant rested rather in repentance, and

in the promise of the Father to pour out the Holy Spirit in
their lives. By the power of the Presence, they would be
able to love God and their neighbors fully and thus, as
Moses and the prophets had said, keep the commandments.

Now we Christians should not expect Jewish students
of the Old Testament to accept readily the idea that this
New Testament episode embodies the central theme of
the Old, but I think it does. They would agree, of course,
that a covenant of reconciliation and moral renewal in
peace and righteousness was the frame upon which the
tapestry of Yahweh's promises from Moses to Malachi are
woven. The covenant of reconciliation lies at the heart of
Old Testament theology; but they still would not place
Jesus at the center of it the way we do. That is a part of
the tragedy of their failure to receive Him as Lord who so
fully incarnates both the law and the prophets.

Moreover, many non-Jewish students will not agree
that this is the place to begin to understand the Hebrew
Scriptures. For these scholars (including, of course, many
evangelical ones) have labored for decades to free the
study of the varied writings of the Old Testament from the
myopic perceptions that have stemmed from a primary
allegiance to the New. They are sure that the Hebrew
Scriptures should speak to us in the first instance on their
own terms, as indeed they did to Jesus' own disciples. The
important point is this: when we really do accept the Old
Testament on its own terms, we are able to see it as a
whole system of promise—of peace, righteousness, and
love, and of the gift and baptism of the Holy Spirit to
enable human beings to realize these ethical hopes.

The proper question, however, for both biblical
scholars and Bible-believing Christians, is a factual one:
did Jesus and the apostles understand correctly when they
asserted that the promise of the hallowing Spirit—of

"grace and peace," poured out on all who would love God and keep His commandments—is the central theme of Old Testament literature?

Was that promise, in fact, the substance of the assurance given to Moses, that one day God would circumcise the hearts of His people so that they could love Him completely? God gave Israel the Law and Moses expounded it in the great series of teachings that comprise the book of Deuteronomy. Towards the end of that book, the Lord agrees with Moses that the people are not really going to be able to obey the Ten Commandments, because they cannot in their fallen condition love God with all their hearts. Such a standard was too high for flesh-and-blood Israelites, despite God's covenants with them and His presence with them, symbolized by the pillar of cloud by day and the pillar of fire by night. But God told Moses to have faith in this promise for the future: "I will circumcise the hearts of this people," He said (using the metaphor drawn from the custom that He had laid upon the Jews), "so they will be able to love me with all their heart" (see Deut. 30:6). John the Baptist, Jesus, and the apostles proclaimed that the hour had come for that promise to be fulfilled. Jesus called it, that first Easter night, "the promise of the Father." He and the apostles thought it the same one that the prophets of Israel had proclaimed.

Were they right? Were the expectations of Pentecost that Jesus awakened in His followers a proper Jewish response to Jeremiah's prophecy of the new covenant, under which God would write His law in our minds and wills? Or to Ezekiel's prophecy that the indwelling of the Spirit would take away our hearts of stone? When the risen Jesus said the word "Shalom," and in the same breath, "receive the Holy Spirit," was He consciously and correctly distilling in five words what Isaiah of Jerusalem had proclaimed, that a king would reign in righteousness and the Spirit be poured upon us from on high; that justice would dwell in the desert and the fruit of righteousness would be peace, bringing quietness and confidence forever?

Certainly Peter's sermon on the day of Pentecost testified this to be what Jesus taught. Peter drew his text not from Isaiah but from Joel, another one of the same generation of prophets: "And it shall come to pass afterward, that I will pour out my spirit on all flesh" (Joel 2:28). And he preached a very political sermon. It declared the heavenly source of the Church of Jesus Christ, inaugurated that day in a Jewish community still beset with the notion that a revolt against Roman rule would prepare the way for the Messiah. Peter said, in effect, that God's way to bring about political righteousness was the outpouring of His Spirit, initially in celebration of the coronation of David's greater Son, who now sat on the throne of eternity. Filled with the hallowing Spirit, Christians became the instruments of justice and love in an evil age, and turned the world upside down.

If the emphasis of the books of Moses, the Psalms, and the prophets is in fact the promise of shalom by the Spirit of God, then Evangelicals are mistaken who think they obey God's Spirit in rationalizing the violence of modern warfare. They are also mistaken to spiritualize the concrete Hebraic meaning of the peace of which the angels sang at Jesus' birth. The angels were singing about shalom—political, economic, moral, and spiritual health—about the whole of what Jesus called blessedness.

Now we have got to respond honestly to that word *shalom.* The Greek word for peace means simply the absence of conflict, which may be a high enough standard for most of us. But the writers of the New Testament were Jews, deeply versed in Scripture. When they said "peace," they had in mind the rich meanings of the

Hebrew word. You can hear those meanings echoed again and again throughout the New Testament, if you listen. The primary one was health, or wholeness, but the secondary meanings include the fulfillment of our highest aspirations, the supply of our temporal needs, loving relationships, and joy. When Jews say, "Shalom, shalom," they mean, may all your needs be supplied. May all your relationships be good. May your wife be healthy and your children wise and strong. May prosperity bless you. May you indeed rest in the house you did not build—as Moses promised Israel when they received the Law at Sinai—and feast from the vineyards you did not plant.

Rare indeed it was for ancient Hebrew writers to use this word detached from its deep roots in the history of God's faithfulness and of their nation's highest spiritual achievements. It signifies both physical and spiritual health, and celebrates the grace of healing. There is a balm in Gilead, there is a great physician who restores wholeness to spirit, soul, and body. When you read the New Testament word "peace" in its actual Hebrew meaning, you cannot play Greek games over the difference between the mind and the body, the ideal and the actual, the individual and society. In Hebrew perception, each of us is one being; and our wholeness or lack of it stems in part from our intimate bonds to other persons. When God speaks to me, He speaks to my whole self, individual and social, spiritual and ethical. As the psalmist put it, "He restores my soul and leads me in the paths of righteousness for His name's sake." Such a restoration to shalom prepares you, my brothers and sisters, for the Christlike vocation of suffering servanthood. God has ordained that your consecration, your faith and witness, will help fulfill His purpose to redeem both humanity and all of nature from the curse of evil. How can you enjoy health when war-ravaged peoples are starving? How can you be whole while your human neighbors on this planet are being dismembered? How can you know anything that you can describe as "peace" if violence stalks the land?

When Jesus said, "My peace I give unto you," his hearers were all Jews. They were in Jerusalem, surrounded by a conspiracy to destroy Him and end their ministry. They understood His words in Hebrew terms, and so must we if we would grasp what they understood. "My peace," Jesus called it, thus saying, There is something added to the quality of grace because God has manifested Himself in me; I have come out of eternity into your time to bring you my shalom. "I give unto you." You do not earn it, but I bring it in grace and give it to you. "Let not your heart be troubled, neither let it be afraid."

Fundamentalists, who honor the unerring truth of Scripture, and Pentecostals, who celebrate the power and presence of the Spirit, may not properly ignore these Old Testament sources of the gospel of the Kingdom that John the Baptist, Jesus, Peter, and Paul proclaimed. "Repent," John the Baptist cried to the Jews in Palestine (quoting another passage from Isa. 40), "Prepare the way for the Lord . . . He will baptize you with the Holy Spirit and with fire" (Luke 3:4,16). The Hebrew Scriptures declare again and again the power of that sanctifying, reconciling, shalom-producing Spirit! Psalm 85:10 reads, "Righteousness and peace kiss each other," and mercy and truth are united.

The unity of the Old and New Testaments is both spiritual and ethical. Justice and holiness, wholeness and spirituality, grace and peace: these are always linked together. Saint Paul's very Jewish greeting, "Grace and peace from God our Father and the Lord Jesus Christ," rebukes the vengefulness and violence of both Christians and Jews in our time. But the practical implications of this ethical and spiritual unity unfold in progressive steps.

The conviction that God's will for humankind was revealed gradually, in successive epochs of salvation history, was not imposed upon evangelical Christians by nineteenth-century social reformers bent on making Scripture speak for the anti-slavery, temperance, peace, and social welfare crusades. That conviction was already widespread in Judaism before Jesus came on the scene announcing that the Spirit of the Lord was upon Him, and that He would preach the gospel of jubilee, and set the captives free. Without the conviction that God unfolds His will progressively to His children, there would have been no room for Hosea and Isaiah to have denounced the substitution of burnt offerings and sacrifices for obedience to the Law, nor for John the Baptist or Jesus to have been recognized instantly as forerunners of the Kingdom. God had from Abraham's day, in Jewish understanding, been bringing His chosen people (and through them the whole world) into the covenant of holiness and love. It was a process then, and it continues so today, though awesomely retarded by our fear that the news of the gospel is too good to be true.

Thus Moses appealed to God's faithful words to Noah, Abraham, and Joseph for proof that the essence of God's law is faithfulness, or love. Hosea, Jeremiah, and Nehemiah extended Moses' teaching about the righteousness of "steadfast love" to challenge the moral failures of their contemporaries, and to promise a better covenant. John the Baptist and Jesus appealed to both Moses and these prophets to proclaim the "fulfillment" of the law.

This powerful word appears in Scripture after Jesus said He had not come "to destroy the Law and the Prophets." Not one jotting of an *i* or one crossing of a *t* will pass away, He said, until all were "fulfilled" (Matt. 5:17,18). Now isn't that puzzling? How do you *fulfill* the Law? We understand fulfilling a promise, but the Law is something we are supposed to *keep*. Many of us attempt to do that by gritting our teeth, clenching our fists, and saying, "I will serve God if it kills me." We chart a rigid course around every pitfall that the devil places in our way in our determination to be a Law-keeping Christian. We must so be, Jesus and Saint Paul both make clear; for the Law, Paul said, is "holy, just, and good." We are not saved by it, but we must aim at keeping it before we can be saved and, in the power of God's grace, live in accordance with it afterwards.

In both Jesus' view and Paul's, however, the Law is not something to be kept, but fulfilled. In what sense, we ask? *Torah,* you see, the Hebrew word for law, means not just a structure of rules to obey. It also means "the story of God's faithfulness." James Sanders, in a wonderful scholarly article on "Torah and Christ," said that the New Testament writers treat the story of Jesus as the last chapter of Torah, of the story of God's faithfulness to His covenants with Israel. The incarnation, atonement, and resurrection of the Divine Son are the climax of that story. They convince us of God's love and lead us, by the inspiration of His Holy Spirit, to that faith through which "the righteousness of the Law is fulfilled in us" (Rom. 8:4).

So in Moses and the prophets the Law of God is a revelation of His love. We obey it by loving Him with all our hearts and loving our neighbors as ourselves. Jesus, quoting Moses, said that all the law and the prophets hang upon the first great commandment, "Love the Lord your God with all your heart and with all your soul and with all your strength" (Deut. 6:5, *NIV*); and the second great commandment, to "love your neighbor as yourself," He quoted also from Moses (Lev. 19:17). Paul and Jesus did not teach different ethical systems, as biblical scholars used to argue. They, with John and the other apostles, described the Law as love, just as Moses did; only they declare that Law and love become one in the right-making power of the Holy Spirit. Thus when Saint Paul begins to urge the Roman Christians not to be conformed to this world but to be transformed by the renewing of their minds so as to be able to demonstrate "the good and perfect will of God," he came shortly to the Ten Commandments, as Jesus always did. The commands, "You shall not commit adultery, you shall not kill, you shall not steal, you shall not covet," and any other divine commandment, Paul wrote, are all summed up in one, "You shall love your neighbor as yourself" (Rom. 13:9).

The Law, then perceived as love, is an implied promise. In it God declares that by His grace we shall be able to fulfill the terms of His covenant. The Old Testament declares everywhere that we are fallen—sinful from the moment of our conception, as the psalmist put it. This is the recurring theme of the early parts of the books of Moses. However, the centrality of Torah in those books, understood as both the rule of life and the story of grace, implies the promise of restoration. I will circumcise your hearts, God says, and you will be able to fulfill the covenant of love and righteousness; I will pour out my Spirit upon you and write my law in your hearts (Deut. 30:6; Ezek. 11:19).

The promises of Jesus are the same—commands clothed with grace. You must be peaceable, He said, and neither scorn nor take vengeance on any person, but walk in love. By His own presence and that of the promised Comforter He assured all who will believe that they would have power to fulfill these commandments. Certainly by the evening of the Last Supper, the apostles knew that they could not be fulfilled by human resolution alone; the Spirit of Christ must become their inward strength.

Indeed, for both Jews and Christians, Isaiah's vision of the Lord who is high and exalted, whose glory fills the earth, illumines the moral promise of all the great formative moments of Hebrew history. Isaiah insisted that the God who was present at the Red Sea is still mightily at work in human history. Like Jeremiah, ancient Judah's great champion of non-resistance, Isaiah declared that the Law of Moses was a revelation of divine love.

Here, again, the Old Testament meanings of a key word, love, determined the use of it by Jesus and the apostles. Read in any good Bible dictionary a detailed exposition of the Hebrew word *Hesed,* and you will find it means faithfulness, or loyalty, as many modern versions of Scripture in fact translate it. This meaning is closely linked to the concept of covenant. It reflects our human experience. What you actually mean by a confession of love to a wife or husband or to a close friend is to promise loyalty, fidelity.

When a young man and a young woman start going out with each other, and everyone else sees the lights in their eyes, this is predictable: some evening they will find themselves silent for a moment, and he will turn to her and say, "I'm not very good at words, but I have to tell you that I love you." I am not sure about what happens in the next moment. In my generation they would have embraced and kissed, and she perhaps would have cried a little. But I know what happens after that, in all cultures and all generations. She asks, "Will you always love me?" If he replies, "Oh, let's not get too serious about things right away," her response is something like, "Then let's not talk about love." She is, of course, right. An old popular song ran, "If you can't say forever, then don't say love."

Our deepest human longing is for relationships with persons we can trust to keep their promises. We seek faithfulness; the tenderness of sexual love is a byproduct of the reverence we feel when commitment is complete. I say to people when I marry them, "Keep your promises. The whole world will be richer if you keep them; but if you break them, we will all be poorer. For all human promises are at risk when you break yours." Alas, our human impulse is to guard ourselves from making promises, and to say only, "I'll try to help you if I possibly can." But God never plays the game of life that way with us. He comes to us from the outset making and keeping promises. I am committed, the Lord says; I will not leave you. The eternal God is your refuge—underneath are His everlasting arms. Even if you are faithless and break the covenant, I will make a new and better one, aimed at restoring you in our divine image. That is what Jesus called the promise of the Father; and He laid down His life to make possible its fulfillment.

Justice, or righteousness, as seen in God's Word and as it should be seen in our lives, flows from such promise-keeping love. Righteousness is the concrete ethical expression of the love of God, given in grace to enable us to be faithful to every human being. If, however, I sequester for my own selfish interest what can make for justice in the world, I am not being faithful. Justice, you see, does not stem from demanding our rights, as if we deserved them. We really do not have by our "just desserts" any rights at all. All that we have are by grace alone. What we can give or bring to the poor and oppressed we have by grace, for love comes from God.

Moreover, our understanding of the practical expression of this "principle of life in Christ Jesus" grows and develops as communities of faith reach new levels of awareness of the human situation. This happens both within and beyond the ages and the cultures represented by the writers of Scripture, even to our own generation. Through the community of faith, as well as our individual consciences, the Holy Spirit reveals to individuals, through Scripture, the relationship of God's law of love to the tasks He calls each believer to undertake. The Lord must teach me things—dare I say it?—that Saint Paul did not know, because he was not called to be a professor of history at an American university in the latter half of the twentieth century. Paul did other and more noble things than I shall ever do, of course; but my task is my own, not his. Likewise, in the Christian community, we must expect unfolding perceptions of the meaning of the gospel of the Kingdom in our time. Certainly, the invention and multiplication of nuclear weapons have stopped many of us who were not pacifists dead in our tracks. We have had to come to grips with issues of war and peace that we did not face up to before.

The next question is, If we know more, may we be assured of grace to act ethically in response to what we know? Here I have to testify that one of the absolutely central themes of Scripture is that as our day is, so shall our strength be. To perceive a challenge to the world and the Kingdom of God is to be entitled to trust the Holy Spirit for grace to be "more than conquerors" over them. In the light of Jesus and the prophets, neither Jews nor Christians should imagine it is proper for them to respond to the threats and challenges that come to them with worldly weapons. "Woe to those who go down to Egypt for help and rely on horses," Isaiah declared (31:1).

Consider, in this light, the tragedy of our own nation's reliance upon weapons and of the German Christians' withdrawal from responsibility, as the Holocaust destroyed European Jewry. At the time a great deal was known in Germany about what was really going on, though people tried then, as many do now, not to think about the unthinkable. Some years ago I spent several months in the archives of the World Council of Churches, reading secret documents sent to its officers from inside Germany during 1942 and 1943. Christian leaders in Geneva knew, through these documents, a great deal of what was going on, and surmised the rest. They did encourage noble actions to help individuals to escape. But neither there nor in Germany did Christians think about a nonviolent crusade against the effort to exterminate Jews. No one proposed that thousands of Christians might lay their bodies against the railroad tracks which bore trainloads of Jews toward their fate at Auschwitz and Treblinka. I am now persuaded that such action was also the real Christian alternative to the firebombing of Dresden and other German cities. The gift of one's life as a peacemaker ought to be at least as sacred in our imagination as the sacrifice of it in making war.

Our great spiritual need today, I think, is to learn to rely upon the Holy Spirit to help us confront in Christian love and faith the nuclear holocaust that now threatens the entire human race. We must take risks, in every temporal sense of that word, of the sort David took in responding to Goliath and, perhaps more to the point, in refusing to murder Saul the king at the cave of Engedi. And we should take courage from what has happened recently in Poland, where the Spirit of God has been working in different ways than we American Protestants often assume He must. Polish Catholics have shaken the Soviet system to its foundation without even brandishing a club, much less firing a gun. I believe that their revolution, still hanging in the balance, to be sure, is a demonstration of the power of the Spirit of God, as well as of their own bravery and longing for freedom.

So, I conclude, how is God speaking to you through the Holy Spirit in regard to what everyone says are "impossible" challenges? America cannot disarm unilaterally, they say; nor can we realistically expect the Soviet Union to join us in disarmament. To this I answer, what we must do to be faithful, God has promised us grace to do. When we commit ourselves in faith to the Holy Spirit's power, we shall be able truly to declare, to a world grimly bracing itself for the extinction of God's creation, "Shalom."

PART II

The Struggle of Christian Consciences

Old Testament Lesson:
A voice of one calling: "In the desert prepare
  the way of the Lord; make straight in the
  wilderness a highway for our God.
Every valley shall be raised up, every mountain
  and hill made low; the rough ground shall
  become level, the rugged places a plain.
And the glory of the Lord will be revealed,
  and all mankind together will see it.
For the mouth of the Lord has spoken" (Isa. 40:3-5, *NIV*).
A shoot will come up from the stump of Jesse;
  from his roots a Branch will bear fruit.
The Spirit of the Lord will rest on him—
  the Spirit of wisdom and of understanding,
  the Spirit of counsel and of power,
  the Spirit of knowledge and of the fear
  of the Lord—and he will delight in the
  fear of the Lord.
He will not judge by what he sees with his eyes,
  or decide by what he hears with his ears;
but with righteousness he will judge the needy,
  with justice he will give decisions for
  the poor of the earth.
He will strike the earth with the rod of his
  mouth; with the breath of his lips he
  will slay the wicked.
Righteousness will be his belt and faithfulness
  the sash around his waist (Isa. 11:1-5, *NIV*).

New Testament Lesson:

As a prisoner for the Lord, then, I urge you to
live a life worthy of the calling you have
received. Be completely humble and gentle;
be patient, bearing with one another in love.
Make every effort to keep the unity of the
Spirit through the bond of peace. There is
one body and one Spirit—just as you were
called to one hope when you were called—one
Lord, one faith, one baptism; one God and
Father of all, who is over all and through all
and in all (Eph. 4:1-6, *NIV*).

Now to him who is able to do immeasurably more
than all we ask or imagine, according to his
power that is at work within us, to him be
glory in the church and in Christ Jesus
throughout all generations, for ever and ever!
Amen (Eph. 3:20-21, *NIV*).

Chapter Five

Pentecost and Peacemaking in a Nuclear Age

by Jim Wallis

On Pentecost evening, May 22, 1983, in the National Cathedral in Washington, D.C., three thousand Christians—clergy and lay leaders—gathered from all over the country. The place was full. It is usually full only at Easter, but this time it was full at Pentecost. It was full of people, full of life, and full of the Spirit.

The music, the dancing, the Scripture, and the sermons were powerful. But mostly we were there to pray—to plead with and beseech the Lord that, as on the first coming of the Holy Spirit, the Spirit of God would be upon us, to unite and enable us to act boldly for the sake of peace.

On Monday, as planned, we gathered again in a church near the Capitol to pray and prepare. The church was again overflowing, and when we came to the street five hundred more people were waiting for us. We proceeded to the Capitol and found one thousand more there.

We had learned two days before that, on the same day as we gathered to pray for peace, the debate and decision on the MX missile would come to the floor of the House and the Senate. So our presence was timely. On that day 242 of us, including more than 100 clergy and members of religious orders, entered the rotunda of the Capitol to pray. We prayed and pleaded for the sake of peace, believing that prayer is now the most important thing we can do and that there are times when we have to move the geography of our prayer to the places where it can be most felt.

We went to pray in the heart of the Capitol building. The police told us that ours was the largest such action in Washington, D.C. since the end of the Viet Nam war. We entered the rotunda carrying loaves of bread and flowers. We planned to pray and sing and read statements of the churches in response to the threat of the nuclear war.

I entered the rotunda not knowing how to begin the liturgy, but the captain of the Capitol police provided a beginning when he said through a bull horn, "It is unlawful to pray in the rotunda of the U.S. Capitol." I responded, "Whether it be lawful or unlawful, we are here to pray for peace." We dropped to our knees and recited the Lord's Prayer, beginning our liturgy of prayers, songs, and statements of the churches in the most appropriate place they had ever been read.

Before the police arrested us, the liturgy of sharing bread and singing gospel songs filled the halls of the Capitol. We found that the acoustics for choir singing in the rotunda are tremendous. Our voices were heard outside and inside. It was nonviolent prayer for the sake of peace occurring right at the time when appropriations were being debated for the MX missile system—one of the most dangerous new weapons systems ever devised by human beings.

We were there because we think that the nuclear arms race is fast approaching a state of crisis that is unparalleled. Yet our political leaders seem unable to respond. It is, therefore, more necessary than ever before for people of faith to take extraordinary actions to stop the superpowers' race toward oblivion. This Pentecost action and other actions across the country represent an escalation of the churches' opposition to the nuclear arms race.

They represent a new stage, a new phase in the formation of a movement of Christian people committed to the abolition of nuclear weapons. Our witness at the Capitol demonstrates, as other actions around the country also do, that large numbers of church people are now willing to make deeper and deeper personal sacrifices, even to risk being arrested and sent to jail, to stop the nuclear arms race.

I have been in jail before, but I have never had such a powerful experience of worship, prayer, and praise of God all night in jail. There is a jail now set aside for "political demonstrators" and we were the first to try it out. Again we found the acoustics wonderful. We sang and prayed and spent the whole night together in a Pentecostal way that was the most powerful thing I had ever known.

The next day in the courtroom, as we were all arraigned, it was touching to hear people share their testimonies. Three-quarters of those arrested had never participated in such an action.

One man said that an Air Force friend of his had explained the deterrence doctrine in this way: deterrence means that if the Russians kill all of our children, we can die with the assurance that our missiles will kill all of their children, too. "I'm here today to plead for the children," he said to the judge. A West German woman with a thick accent said that when the Americans came to Nuremberg after World War II, "They told us that we had a personal responsibility to stand up and say no to the holocaust that took place. I am here in the rotunda today to say no." Another person said, "I have nothing to say except that Jesus is Lord."

But why this historical moment for this kind of action? A few days before Palm Sunday in 1983, President Reagan spoke to the nation about his military plans and proposals[1]—two trillion dollars over the next five years for the development of a whole new generation of nuclear weapons systems including the MX and the missiles to be deployed in Europe. These are counterforce weapons, the first-strike weapons that many of us have heard about for such a long time. These weapons bring dangerous destabilization and increased fear on every side. As many observers have put it, "When first-strike weapons are in place, nuclear war will have a hair trigger."

As always in all the clamor for higher and higher levels of military spending, the cries of the poor are simply never heard. The numbers of the hungry, the homeless, and the unemployed continue to swell. As the arms race escalates, the suffering of the poor multiplies.

Every Saturday morning in my neighborhood, the line for food forms at 6:00 A.M., even though our food line does not open until 8:30 A.M. In line are people who have not been in such lines before—mostly families, women and children. They wait in line for packages of food. They wait in line a mile and a half from the White House, where decisions are made to fund the nuclear arms race at their expense.

In March of 1983, in his speech before the National Association of Evangelicals, Reagan described the Soviet Union as the focus of evil in a modern world and portrayed the struggle between the United States and the Soviet Union as the ultimate moral clash between right and wrong, good and evil.[2] When I heard that speech, the words of Jesus rang in my ears. Why is it that we see the specks in our brother's eye but never the logs in our own? Why do we think we are so righteous, so morally superior to the Soviets? Why is it that we cannot see ourselves and the Soviets the way most of the world's poor people see us?

My neighbors are not afraid of the Soviet Union. They are more afraid of the decisions made in the corridors of power in Washington, D.C. The real struggle in our world today is not between East and West but between North and South, rich and poor, powerful and powerless, those who are armed to the teeth and those who are victims of their weapons. Those at the top of the world system— both white superpowers—are beneficiaries of a world system, a world economic order that, in the end, is not too much more than organized theft from poor people. This is how most of the world's people see this arms race.

In that same speech we heard plans for a new program to deploy missile defense systems in outer space, thereby threatening to set off another round in the arms race competition. One can see, again, each side seeking to match the other's defensive capacity while pursuing new offensive systems and then new defensive systems. We call it arms control. Every new weapons system now being offered in the United States Congress is justified in the name of arms control. We are told that we need the MX missile and every other missile for arms control.

The arms race will not be ended by a new balance of terror. In fact the concepts of balance and deterrence are the engines of the arms race. They propel it further along. The arms race will not be ended by a new balance but by a new breakthrough, a new moral sensibility, a new moral understanding and commitment among people of faith to live and act in different ways.

The fundamental deadly error of trying to end the arms race by building more weapons instead of dismantling present ones has never been more clear. The lectionary for Palm Sunday following Reagan's speech included the passage about Jesus' response as He drew nearer to Jerusalem. He wept over the city and spoke words that I think go right to the heart of our situation. "Would that even today you knew the things that make for peace" (Luke 19:41,42).

In recent months and years, the church has proclaimed its opposition to the nuclear arms race both in official statements and grassroots actions. The government has not responded to this plea for peace from the churches. The race for superiority continues and now enters a new and more dangerous era.

It is increasingly clear that the arms race will not be ended by the use of traditional, political channels alone. Important legislative initiatives like the nuclear freeze resolution deserve, I think, our support. But it will undoubtedly take a deeper level of commitment and sacrifice to end the perilous threat to human life and God's creation than we are now confronting. Indeed, it will take a powerful movement of conscience and direct action at least as strong as the civil rights movement, the abolitionist struggle, or Gandhi's struggle to free India. For that kind of movement, the vision and resources of biblical faith will be required. The struggle to abolish nuclear weapons must be rooted in a spiritual commitment. The churches could lead the way in a disciplined, prayerful movement of nonviolent action. Never has the alternative vision and leadership of the church been more required than now.

It is indeed an historical movement. It is opportune not only for political reasons, but it is also a crucial time for the Church. The time to speak out is now. For these reasons Christian lay people and clergy from all over the country entered the rotunda of the Capitol to pray. In coming to the rotunda, we were not acting against the Congress but against decisions to continue an arms race and officially abandon the poor.

The Bible would speak strong words to us right now—stronger words than we want to hear. But instead of listening to the Bible we have accumulated many possessions and turned away from the cries of the poor. Instead of listening to the Bible we have built walls of hatred, hostility, and fear between the peoples of the world and now have amassed great arsenals by which we can destroy each other. Now the momentum of our technology, the genius of our science, and the human capacity for evil have combined to bring us to the precipice of total war. Our weapons are now ultimate, and we and our children, and the creation itself, will not likely survive their use.

How could we have even imagined it? How could we have imagined the end of everything—music, art, literature, science, laughter, tears, human love and pain, the past, the whole future, all the living creatures God has made, and all God's people? Just to imagine it, to contemplate this kind of destruction, is an awful sin.

With our nuclear weapons we have taken the power of life and death into our hands. We have tried to take the place of God. Therefore, the nuclear arms race is a rebellion, a blasphemy, an idolatry, a sin against God. That is why people of faith must devote their lives, their energy to understanding what God might have us do. This sin is not only against the earth. This sin is against heaven itself.

The words of Jesus must ring in our ears now as we have never heard them before. "Blessed are the peacemakers: for they shall be called the children of God" (Matt. 5:9, *KJV*). Some succumb to hysteria, hate, and fear. Others rush to war. But those who would make peace are called God's very own children.

"You have heard that it was said, 'You shall love your neighbor and hate your enemies.' But I say to you," says Jesus, "Love your enemies" (Matt. 5:43,44). Why? Because that is what God did for us.

I learned as a young boy growing up in the evangelical church that we were all enemies of God by our sin, hate, and rebellion, but that God loved us enough to send Jesus to live and die to save us, to reconcile us back to God and to each other and to show us the way to live. Do not let anyone tell you that peace is a political question only. Jesus died for the peace that we have come to understand in these days—peace with God, peace with our neighbor, peace, yes, even with our enemy, all won at the cost of Jesus' life.

A group of Scandinavian women made a pilgrimage recently to Minsk in the Soviet Union. All along the way they talked to Soviet people who responded to their pleas for peace with words like this: "We want peace, too, but you know how the Americans are. We simply can't trust them. We can't let our guard down for a moment. If we showed weakness they would overwhelm us. The only thing the Americans understand is power." The words sound like a tape recording. Just interchange "Russians" and "Americans" and you can hear it played over and over in every American and Soviet city.

If there is one thing we must understand it is that whoever is right and whoever is wrong, the Soviets are as afraid of us as we are of them. Our respective national fears have become mere projections of each other. Like most fears, some are real and some are imagined. Both sides have behaved in ways that cause the other side to be legitimately afraid. Both sides have allowed their fears to escalate out of all proportion. Both sides paint worst-case scenarios, and our fears have now made us contemplate ultimate violence against each other. Unless our fears are dealt with, they will certainly destroy us.

The admonition of Jesus to love our enemies is believable only as long as our enemies are general and unspecified. But when they are identified as Russians or Iranians or Cubans or whomever the government names as our adversary of the year, the statement becomes outrageous. "Love your enemies" is admired as the word of the Lord until it is suggested that it means you cannot at the same time love your enemies and plot their annihilation.

But what about the Russians? Even in our churches that continues to be the most commonly asked question when one begins to talk about the arms race. Even in our churches the Soviet threat gets more attention than the words of Jesus.

The question may be the right one. But perhaps we are asking the question in the wrong way. What about the Russians? What about the Russian people and their children? What would become of them in a nuclear exchange? They are among the hundreds of millions of God's children whom we seem quite ready to make expendable in the name of such lofty phrases as "freedom, democracy, and national security." The question we should be asking is, What has become of us? What does it say about a people when they are prepared to commit what must be called mass murder? For some actions, there are no reasons good enough.

Try to imagine Hiroshima. Try to imagine 1,600,000 Hiroshimas. That is our nuclear capacity today. How is it that we have come so far? I think, very simply, we have come so far by not looking into the faces of the people of Hiroshima and by not looking into the faces of those whom we now call our enemies.

An Israeli soldier during the Beirut war said, "It's so hard when I'm up close. I can see the faces of the people. I can't bring myself to kill them. But when I'm farther away just shooting artillery shells, then I can do it; only when I can't see their faces." A young American in a missile silo, his finger on the nuclear button said, "I don't know if I could kill anybody up close. This way I never have to see who my missile hits."

We do not see the faces either. Our missiles are aimed at the Soviet threat, at the Russian system, at godless communism, at the enemy. But our missiles will hit people, families, and children, hundreds and millions of them just like at Nagasaki and Hiroshima. Missiles do not kill systems. Missiles only kill people. And missiles hit churches and synagogues and millions of brothers and sisters who share with us a common faith and a common Lord.

It is an historic irony that there were Catholics on the bomber crew that bombed the city of Nagasaki, the city of Japan with the largest Catholic population. Ground zero that day for the Nagasaki bomb was the spire of the Catholic cathedral. And on that day hundreds of worshipers were killed as well as two whole orders of Catholic women religious.

The faces of Hiroshima and Nagasaki have been looking at us for thirty-eight years and they refuse to turn away from our eyes as we have turned away from theirs. They look at us quietly, patiently, and earnestly; they will look at us until we look back at them and see what we have done, what the fate of the earth will be unless we turn away from our present course. No longer can we turn away from our own flesh in the name of national security or any other name. We must say to ourselves and our nation's leaders, "In the name of God, look at the faces. Look at the faces."

Some will say that we are naive and unrealistic in the face of nuclear war. But I would say with the world on the edge of nuclear conflict, who must now be called naive?

Which policy must now be called unrealistic? To believe that nuclear weapons can defend and save anything or anyone is naive and unrealistic. That is the great illusion that has blinded our eyes and hardened our hearts. We must see now before it is too late. Unless we see a neighbor now in the face of our enemy, we have no future.

Are we evangelical Christians or are we not? Are the words of Jesus more important to us than moral philosophy, than complicated theological discourse or the rationales of national security? The world is waiting to see how much the words of Jesus mean to those who name His name. Conversion is to see the face of the enemy. It is to see the face of Jesus in the ones whom we target for destruction. "As you did it to one of the least of these," the poor, the forgotten, the marginal and, yes, the enemy, "you did it to me" (Matt. 25:40).

In the face of nuclear war, we are being led back to Jesus and His way of the cross. Virtually no one denies the nonviolence of Jesus. But most often His way of suffering love has been ignored or dismissed as irrelevant to political struggle. What we are now finding is that the cross of Jesus Christ is not only the means of our salvation, but it is also intended to be the pattern for our discipleship. That fact has as much political meaning as personal significance in our lives. The historical crisis we face and the clear command of the One whom we call Lord requires that we take up the cross as the means of seeking justice and making peace in our dangerous situation.

A central reality to the arms race is that by United States domestic laws it is all perfectly legal. Many Christians have challenged nuclear weapons on the basis of moral or international law, but neither argument has ever been accepted in a U.S. court. Not only does the law of the land make clear that there is no illegality in the escalation of nuclear weapons, it also upholds the arms race by collecting and appropriating our tax dollars for nuclear weapons, by shrouding decision-making regarding nuclear policy in a veil of secrecy, and by keeping people outside of the fences and boundaries of nuclear facilities with the sign No Trespassing.

Increasing numbers of Christians are finding that a serious commitment to peacemaking will ultimately lead them to confront the question of the law itself. To say no to nuclear weapons means to say no to the habits and the assumptions and the laws that make their existence possible.

The existence and proliferation of nuclear weapons has become for us what slavery was for Christians in the nineteenth century. A clear moral choice has emerged that now supercedes all complex moral argumentation. The connection between nuclear weapons and slavery was for us at Sojourners a natural one because of our evangelical heritage and tradition.

In preaching the gospel, I have learned that sin must be publicly addressed and the salvation available in Christ made concrete to each and every age. Never has the gospel of peace been more needed than now. We must take great strength and courage from the abolitionists of the last century because it was their burning faith and tireless commitment against slavery that created the spiritual force that toppled that hideous institution. At first, they were thought to be idealists, utopian dreamers, and even fools. Few could imagine a world without slavery. The whole economy, it was said, rested upon it.

But the revivalists who traveled the length and breadth of this country would not be satisfied with mere reform or moderate improvements in the situation. They demanded nothing less than the abolition of slavery. It took thirty or forty years of perseverance and sacrifice and even suffering. A world without slavery could not be visualized at first, except through the eyes of faith. But because of their clear and unrelenting vision, others also came to see. And through faith and prayer, sweat, blood, and tears, a new day of freedom dawned.

Our situation is more perilous than that. We have less and less time. The nuclear spring is more tightly wound every day. The struggle for peace will be at least as arduous and costly as the battle against slavery. The stakes have never been higher.

Today I believe that a revival of faith to bring spiritual transformation is the best hope we have of ending the arms race and abolishing nuclear weapons. That revival has already begun, and the key to it is the recognition of the nuclear crisis as a spiritual one. The nuclear danger is becoming an occasion of fresh conversion for a growing number of people in the churches. Opposition to nuclear weapons is increasingly being seen as a matter of obedience to Jesus Christ.

A new abolitionist movement is emerging based on a new level of prayer, preaching, commitment, and sacrifice. The conversion of whole sectors of the churches to peacemaking is unprecedented and is the most visible sign of spiritual renewal in our day. There were prophets among us who saw, early on, the implications of all this and began to alert the rest of the Church. But now church leaders are speaking out, taking stands in direct opposition to their own government. Whole churches and congregations are being mobilized for the sake of peace. Ordinary Christians are making life-changing decisions that are costing them something. The God of the Bible is being rediscovered as the Author of life, and His Son as the Prince of Peace.

I believe that in many ways only the Church can stop the arms race now. Without the consent and support of the churches, the arms race could not continue. The greatest political hope we have would be for the churches of East and West, North and South, to regain that biblical vision of the Body of Christ which knows no boundaries of race, nation, or ideology but lives in the world as a community of reconciliation. The Church could lead the way to peace. The people of God could unite to create the kind of moral force to stop the insanity of the world's political rulers on both sides. The Christians could withdraw their consent, refuse to collaborate, obstruct war-making plans and point to alternatives.

But the way to peace will be the way of the cross for those who choose to be peacemakers. It was for Jesus, and it will be for all those who would follow in His path. If the churches are to provide leadership for peace, they will certainly rediscover the cross. The cross will again become the sign of our lives.

The sign of the nuclear age is the bomb. The sign of Christ is the cross. The bomb is the great countersign to the cross. It arrogantly threatens to undo the work the cross has done. In the cross, all things are reconciled; in the bomb, all things are destroyed. In the cross, violence is defeated; in the bomb, violence is victorious. In the cross, evil has been overcome; in the bomb, evil has dominion. In the cross, death is swallowed up; in the bomb, death reigns supreme.

Which will hold sway in our time? Will we live under the sign of the cross or under the sign of the bomb? And, finally, which sign will the church choose for its life? The greatest evangelistic question before us today is, Will the church be converted from the bomb to the cross?

We have a Caesar church in this land. But we also have the church of Jesus Christ. When Ronald Reagan went to Orlando to speak to the National Association of Evangelicals, he was looking for a church for Caesar. Evangelicals must answer the question, What kind of church do we want to be? The time has come for an evangelical decision. The time has come for an altar call in the face of nuclear war.

On Pentecost we remember that the disciples had been hiding behind closed doors, after Jesus was killed, for fear of the authorities. They were afraid that they might be next. Their minds were not preoccupied with the preaching of the gospel, with the good news of the Kingdom of God. Their minds were preoccupied with how to save their own skins. Most of us can identify with that feeling.

But we all know what happened next. The tomb and the bonds of death could not hold Him. The Roman seal was broken. The guards were scattered, the stone was rolled away, and the resurrected Christ, conquering sin and death, appeared to the astonished disciples, and it changed their lives. He was with them again, comforting, exhorting, strengthening, instructing, staying with them for forty days, speaking of the Kingdom of God. Then He left them, ascended into heaven and told them to return to Jerusalem and wait for the coming of the Spirit.

On Pentecost, the Bible says, they were all together, and suddenly the Spirit came with a sound like a mighty rushing wind that filled the whole house. Tongues of fire rested on each one, and they were filled with the Holy Spirit. They began to speak in many tongues of the mighty works of God.

Peter, the leader, who had denied Jesus three times, stood to repeat the words of Joel, the promise of God to "pour out my Spirit upon all flesh," young and old, men and women (Acts 2:17,18). Peter preached with boldness and testified to Jesus, confronting the Jerusalem crowds and the authorities with the gospel.

The Bible says three thousand responded and entered the community of faith while signs and wonders were done. All who believed had everything in common. They sold their goods and possessions and gave to the poor. They shared bread, fellowship, and prayer with glad and generous hearts praising God. And the Lord added to their numbers.

The most remarkable thing is that they had been so afraid. But then they saw Jesus, received the Holy Spirit, and came down from the upper room to the streets to proclaim the gospel.

Then they began to get in trouble with the authorities. Acts recounts incident after incident of threats, harassment, beatings, imprisonment, and martyrdom. But these disciples were now filled with the Spirit and faced their suffering for the joy and sake of Christ. One of their enemies testified against them in court saying, "These men and women have turned the world upside down." Just as those apostles were empowered on that first Pentecost to go out and boldly preach the gospel of Jesus Christ, so we hope in our day to be moved by the Spirit again—to proclaim that the Good News is alive in our day, that the gospel can work, that the gospel is strong, that the foolishness of God is stronger than the wisdom of this world.

I believe the day has come for the Church to stand in the way of nuclear war, to refuse to cooperate any longer with its preparations, to place its faith and life as an obstacle to the arms race. For that we will need the power of the Spirit.

What is required of us today is a love that we are not strong enough to give with our own strength. To love as strongly, as deeply, as sacrificially as we must, we will need the help of the Holy Spirit.

On that first Pentecost there was a rush of mighty wind, a bold proclamation of the gospel, many conversions, the creation of community, the establishment of the Church, and justice for the poor. And today, also, a new wind is blowing—the wind of the Spirit. Conversion is happening again. Lives are being transformed and community established. A new love for the poor is growing in the churches, and a whole new commitment to peacemaking is developing. The only question is, Are we going to be part of it? Are we going to come forward and stand with what the Spirit is doing in our day?

We say, Come Holy Spirit. We need you now more than ever. Remove our fears, strengthen our wobbling knees. Straighten our bent backs. Refresh our tired bodies. Heal us, cleanse us. Replace our hearts of stone with hearts of flesh. Oh, Holy Spirit, course through our veins and empower our lives. "Melt us, mold us, fill us, use us, Spirit of the Living God. Fall afresh on us." Come Holy Spirit. Come Holy Spirit.

Notes
1. This is a reference to President Reagan's televised address to the nation on March 23, 1983.
2. This is a reference to President Reagan's speech before the National Association of Evangelicals in Orlando, Florida on March 8, 1983.

Chapter Six

The Way of the Cross in the Nuclear Age

by Ronald J. Sider

For millennia, humanity has sought security through violence. Almost all societies have hoped that state-of-the-art weapons would deter aggressive neighbors. Sometimes it worked for short intervals, but seldom for long.

Ever more sophisticated technology provided ever more deadly weapons. Clubs gave way to longbows, chariots to tanks, and cannons to nuclear missiles—and lasers. Very seldom and never for long did the weapons improve anyone's security. Ever more deadly weapons merely guaranteed that the next battle would destroy even more people.

Today we stand at the end of that long violent road littered with the broken bodies of millions of our best sons and daughters. State-of-the-art nuclear weapons give us the power to destroy the planet. Increasingly, people in the best positions to know, like Admiral Rickover, warn that unless we get rid of nuclear weapons we will destroy ourselves. Every new generation of nuclear weapons increases the danger, shortens the nuclear trigger, and decreases our security. The best insight of conventional wisdom is suicidal madness. We are at an impasse.

The only way to avoid disaster is to take a different path. Security through violence has never worked well; it will not work at all today. Martin Luther King was right: "Today the choice is no longer between violence and nonviolence. It is either nonviolence or nonexistence."

Christian history, I believe, encourages us to reexamine the nonviolent alternative. The Just-War tradition represents a sustained, courageous attempt to restrain the evil of warfare. Unfortunately that tradition has not been able to prevent a long tragic history of European wars in which Christians slaughtered their brothers and sisters in Christ by the millions. The history of warfare in Christendom makes a mockery of the biblical doctrine of the unity of Christ's body.

In spite of the careful criteria of the Just-War tradition, societal pressure and nationalistic sentiment have almost always prompted Christians to fight in every war that occurred. If Allied opposition to Hitler is the classic example of a Just War, then Hitler's attacks provide the classic example of an unjust war. But the overwhelming majority of German Christians, both Protestant and Catholic, failed to say no to this unjust war. Does not the consistent pattern of nationalistic rationalization suggest that the hope of faithfully applying the Just-War criteria rests on an optimistic view of human nature? Might not consistent nonviolence be a more realistic response to this essential human sinfulness?

The nonviolent witness of the early Church strengthens the case for exploring this alternative. Modern historical scholarship has discovered that until the fourth century there is not a single existing Christian writing which defends or allows Christian participation in any form of lethal violence, whether abortion, capital punishment, or war. All known Christian writings dealing with this subject in the first three centuries claim that Jesus' summons to love our enemies means that Christians should reject the way of lethal violence. At this moment in history when the violent road has led to the very precipice of global suicide, the peaceful witness of the early Church encourages us to look again at the claim that the nonviolent cross of Christ points the way beyond the present impasse.

"Peace among men on earth," the angels sang when God's Son came into our midst as a helpless infant. The Jews of Jesus' day waited breathlessly for the Messianic Age of peace, long foreseen by the prophets (see Isa. 2:4; 9:5-8; 11:6,9). But they expected that peaceful age only after the Messiah had violently overthrown the Roman oppressors who ruled Palestine.

The Babe of Bethlehem did claim to be the Messiah. He announced that the long-expected Messianic Age of peace and righteousness was indeed breaking into the present evil age in His own person and work. But He disappointed passionate nationalists with His summons to love enemies, even hated Roman oppressors. He grounded this radical demand in the very nature of God who also loves His enemies. Indeed, as Messiah and Son of God, He claimed divine authority to dispense forgiveness. And He pointed to His death as the key to this astounding configuration of blasphemous claims and revolutionary ideas.

After the Resurrection, His followers continued to teach and live Jesus' nonviolent way. They also offered to a divided, broken world a new community of peace where hostile dividing walls between Jews and Gentiles, slaves and masters were crumbling. Like Jesus, they grounded their radical message and revolutionary social order in the atonement. They loved their enemies because God Himself had reconciled His sinful enemies when His Incarnate Son died on the cross for our sins. Jesus' self-sacrificial death for others was for them both the unrepeatable ground of unconditional acceptance before God, and also the central ethical clue about how to treat both friend and foe. Those who want to imitate the heavenly Father who loved a sinful world so much that He gave His only Son should be ready to take the way of the cross in a violent, fallen world.

Before Easter, this way of love seemed impossible, even to the disciples like Peter. But the Resurrection and Pentecost removed all doubt that the new Messianic Age had truly invaded this old age. In the power of the Spirit, Jesus' peaceful approach to enemies became a present possibility.

That, in brief, is the heart of the biblical case for nonviolence I want to develop.

That apocalyptic, messianic expectation was widespread and intense among the nationalistic Jews of the first century A.D. is hardly surprising. Almost everyone longed for the dawning of the new age when the Messiah would come to end the rule of the hated foreign oppressors. Given the common assumption of all messianic expectation that the Messiah would end Roman rule, the Romans naturally took a dim view of messianic claims.

And they had good reason to be worried. When Herod the Great died, just after Jesus' birth, three different messianic pretenders provoked armed rebellion. The Roman governor of Syria came to Jerusalem and crucified two thousand rebels. A man named Judas, who was probably a founder of the Zealots a few years later, attacked an arse-

nal of Herod's three miles from Jesus' hometown of Nazareth. Jewish Palestine during the reign of Herod had great
messianic expectations and had become a political and religious tinderbox.

In A.D. 6, when Judea became a Roman province, an
underground organization of violent, nationalistic revolutionaries emerged. The Zealots were full of ardent zeal for
the law and intense messianic expectation. Deeply religious, they believed that God would intervene to usher in
the new age if they could provoke a popular rebellion
against Rome. According to the Zealots, slaying the godless was a religious duty.

The Zealots's mixture of fiery nationalism, religious
zeal, and concern for justice had significant popular appeal.
In a setting of widespread oppression, their call to abolish
the subjection of debtors, to break up large estates, and
liberate slaves was popular. In A.D. 6, Judas attracted
many followers and a popular uprising was only narrowly
averted. Partially suppressed, the Zealots operated as
guerrilla bands from their strongholds in the caves of the
Judaean desert. Occasionally, they raided Jerusalem, kid-
napping prominent persons to exchange for prisoners.
Finally, in A.D. 66, the Zealots achieved sufficient support
to conquer Jerusalem and begin the Jewish War. The result
was the total destruction of the city.

In Jesus' time, the question of violent revolution was a
burning issue—probably the political issue of the day. And
the Zealot answer was popular.

The German New Testament scholar, Martin Hengel,
summarizes this background of imperialist violence, foreign oppression, and violent nationalism so full of surprising parallels to the injustice, violence and nationalism of
our own time:

For the unsophisticated Jewish population, it was

almost entirely a history of oppressive exploita-
tion, wars of indescribable brutality and disappointed hopes. The rule of Herod and his sons and
the corrupt regime of the procurators—Pilate not
the least among them—had made the situation in
Jewish Palestine so intolerable that apparently
only three possibilities remained: armed revolutionary resistance, more or less opportunistic
accommodation to the establishment—leaving
open the possibility of mental reservations—and
patient passive endurance.[1]

It was into that maelstrom of oppression, violence and
intense messianic expectation that Jesus of Nazareth
stepped to proclaim and incarnate a fourth possibility—the
way of suffering servanthood and unconditional love for
enemies grounded in God's unmerited mercy toward sinners.

No image more powerfully contrasts Jesus' peaceful,
messianic conception with violent contemporary expectations than does that of the suffering servant. Popular Jewish thought hoped for a war-like, Davidic Messiah who
would destroy the heathen oppressors. The early Church
taught that the Jewish messianic hope had been fulfilled in
the humble suffering servant foreseen in Isaiah 53. This
Old Testament passage spoke of a lowly servant who
would suffer rather than kill. In his careful scholarly study,
Professor J. Jeremias concludes that from the beginning
the early Christians saw Jesus as the fulfillment of Isaiah's
"servant of God."[2] Jesus Himself seemed to view His
death as well as His life in terms of Isaiah 53.

Jesus claimed to be the Messiah—albeit such a different Messiah that everyone was astonished and perplexed.
As messianic Son of Man, He demonstrated the presence

of the Kingdom in unconventional, astonishing forgiveness of blatant sinners. Even more perplexing and unorthodox was His assertion that as Messiah He would suffer and die for others, even enemies, rather than kill and destroy them.

Only in this context can we adequately understand Jesus' important teaching about peacemaking. It is the One who comes as Israel's true Messiah, but then totally rejects all violent messianic visions, who rebukes Peter for using the sword. It is the One who faces the burning political question of His day and rejects violence as the way to usher in the messianic Kingdom who says, "Turn the other cheek." It is the Messiah whose Kingdom has already begun in dramatic acts of divine forgiveness who says, "Love your enemies . . . so that you may be sons of your Father who is in heaven." In both actions and words, Jesus rejects lethal violence.

Jesus chose nonviolent means at crucial points in His career. At the triumphal entry Jesus clearly disclosed His nonviolent messianic conception. Both Matthew (21:5) and John (12:15) quote Zechariah 9:9–10 to underline their belief that Jesus' action fulfilled this Old Testament prophecy. Modern commentators agree that Jesus consciously chose to fulfill the eschatological prophecy of Zechariah 9:9,10 precisely because it depicted a humble peaceful Messiah, riding on a humble donkey rather than a war horse. This is the messianic picture Jesus chose to fulfill.

In the final crisis, He persisted in His rejection of the sword. He rebuked Peter for attacking those who came to arrest Him: "All who take the sword will perish by the sword" (Matt. 26:52). Not even the defensive sword dare be used. It is significant that Jesus' rebuke to Peter gives a general reason for not using the sword, not just an objection to use in this special case.

Similarly, Jesus informed Pilate that His Kingdom was

not of this world *in one specific way*—namely that His followers do not use violence. "My kingship is not of this world; if my kingship were of this world, my servants would fight, that I might not be handed over to the Jews; but my kingship is not from the world" (John 18:36). Jesus obviously did not mean that the messianic kingdom He had begun had nothing to do with this world. That would have contradicted the kingdom values He announced. And it would have made nonsense of the very prayer He taught His disciples: "Thy kingdom come *on earth* as it is in heaven."

Jesus not only lived the way of nonviolence, He also taught it. Matthew 5:38-48 is the central passage:

> You have heard that it was said, "An eye for an eye and a tooth for a tooth." But I say unto you, Do not resist one who is evil. But if any one strikes you on the right cheek, turn to him the other also; and if any one would sue you and take your coat, let him have your cloak as well; and if any one forces you to go one mile, go with him two miles. Give to him who begs from you, and do not refuse him who would borrow from you. You have heard that it was said, "You shall love your neighbor and hate your enemy." But I say to you, Love your enemies and pray for those who persecute you, so that you may be sons of your Father who is in heaven; for he makes his sun rise on the evil and on the good, and sends rain on the just and on the unjust. For if you love those who love you, what reward have you? Do not even the tax collectors do the same? And if you salute only your brethren, what more are you doing than others? Do not even the Gentiles do the same? You, therefore, must be perfect, as your heavenly Father is perfect.

To a people so oppressed by foreign conquerors that repeatedly over the previous two centuries they had resorted to violent rebellion, Jesus gave the unprecedented command: "Love your enemies." The New Testament scholar Martin Hengel believes that Jesus probably formulated this command to love one's enemies in conscious contrast to the teaching and practice of the Zealots. Thus Jesus was pointedly rejecting one currently popular political method in favor of a radically different approach.

Jesus' command to love one's enemies is in direct contrast to current widespread views that Jesus summarizes in verse 43: "You have heard that it was said, 'You shall love your neighbor and hate your enemy.'" The first part of this verse is a direct quotation from Leviticus 19:18: "You shall love your neighbor as yourself."

But who is the neighbor? The first part of Leviticus 19:18 indicates that the neighbor is a "son of our own people." This was the normal Jewish viewpoint. New Testament scholar John Piper, in his extensive study of pre-Christian thinking about love for neighbor, shows that in Jewish thought the neighbor that one was obligated to love was normally understood to be a fellow Israelite.[3] Thus love for neighbor had clear ethnic, religious limitations. A different attitude toward Gentiles was expected. Seldom, however, did the Old Testament command or sanction hatred of foreigners or enemies. But Jewish contemporaries of Jesus did! The Zealots believed that "slaying of the godless enemy out of zeal for God's cause was a fundamental commandment, true to the rabbinic maxim: 'Whoever spills the blood of one of the godless is like one who offers a sacrifice.'" And the Qumran community's Manual of Discipline urged people to "love all the sons of light . . . and . . . hate all the sons of darkness.[4]

Jesus was radically different. Loving those who love you (v. 46), Jesus says, is relatively easy—even great sinners like tax collectors can do that. In fact even the pagan Gentiles act kindly toward the people in their own ethnic group. Jesus totally rejects that kind of ethnic or religious limitation on love.

For the members of Jesus' beginning messianic kingdom, neighbor love must extend beyond the limited circle of the people of Israel, beyond the limited circle of the new people of God! This text says explicitly what the parable of the Good Samaritan (Luke 10:29-37) suggests. All people everywhere are neighbors to Jesus' followers and therefore are to be actively loved. And that includes enemies— even violent, oppressive foreign conquerors!

The extreme difficulty of actually implementing this command has led to many attempts to weaken its radical demand. Martin Luther restricted the application of these verses on love of enemies to the personal sphere, and denied their application to the Christian in public life, saying that in that case one did "not have to ask Christ about your duty." The emperor supplied the ethic for public life. However, the exegetical context demonstrates that Jesus clearly intended the command to apply to the public sphere. In verses 39-41 of Matthew 5, Jesus had discussed issues that pertained to the public sphere of the legal system and the authorized demands of the Roman rulers.

When Jesus rejects the principle of "an eye for an eye" He is transcending a basic legal principle of the Mosaic law (e.g. Exod. 21:24). Jesus was dealing with a fundamental principle of Jewish and other near-Eastern legal systems. Instead of demanding what the law permitted, namely retaliation to a corresponding degree against someone who had caused damage, Jesus commanded a loving response governed by the needs of the other person. One should even submit to further damage and suffering rather than exact equal pain or loss from the unfair, guilty aggressor. In no way dare the other person's response govern one's action. Matthew 5:40 ("If any one would sue you and take your coat, let him have your cloak as well") clearly speaks of how one should respond in the public arena of the judicial system.

Verse 41 ("If any one force you to go one mile, go with him two miles") deals with how to respond to Roman rulers who demand forced labor. The verb translated as "force" is a technical term used to refer to the requisition of services by civil and military authorities. Josephus used the word to speak of compulsory carrying of military supplies. The Roman rulers could and did demand that civilians in conquered lands perform such services upon demand. Thus they had the right to demand that Simon of Cyrene carry Jesus' cross (Matt. 27:32). It is hardly surprising that the Zealots urged Jews to refuse this kind of forced labor. Jesus, on the other hand, condemns the Zealots' violent, angry response, even to the Romans' unjust demands.

But this raises a pressing problem. Is Jesus forbidding all forms of resistance to evil? Some forms of coercion would seem to be fully compatible with love and respect for the other person as a free moral agent, while others would not. One can lovingly use coercion in the home with children, in the church in discipline with brothers or sisters, and in the marketplace with economic boycotts, and still respect the other person's freedom to say no and accept the consequences. Lethal violence is different. One can engage in all the forms of nonlethal coercion just mentioned and at the same time appeal to the other person as a free moral agent responsible to God to choose to repent and change. When one engages in lethal violence, that is impossible.

When Jesus said, "Do not resist one who is evil," did He mean to forbid all forms of resistance? Jesus' own actions demonstrate that He did not mean to forbid nonviolent opposition to evil. He constantly opposed evil persons in a forthright, vigorous fashion. For example, He unleashed blistering attacks on the Pharisees (Matt. 23:13-33, as an example). Nor was Jesus nonresistant when He cleansed the Temple! If Matthew 5:39 means that all forms of resistance to evil are forbidden, then Jesus contradicted His own teaching. Jesus certainly did not kill the money-changers. Indeed, we doubt that He even used His whip on them. But He certainly resisted their evil in a dramatic act of nonviolent resistance. Nor did Jesus silently submit to aggression at His trial when a soldier unjustly struck Him on the cheek (John 18:19-24).

What then does Matthew 5:39 mean? It means four very challenging things: (1) that one should not respond to an evil person by placing him in the category of enemy; (2) that one should not retaliate, but rather respond according to the needs of the offending person, regardless of his offensive attitude or action; (3) that regardless of the offending person's response, one must continue to love because love does not depend on reciprocity; (4) that one should act thus even at great personal cost. Thus, the good of the other person, not one's own needs or rights, is decisive. Jesus rejected all retaliation. Instead of hating or retaliating, Jesus' followers are lovingly to respond in terms of the need of the other person.

Until the time of Constantine in the fourth century, all Christian writing reflects the belief that Jesus clearly and explicitly forbade Christians to participate in war and capital punishment. Since that time, however, many Christians have thought otherwise.

Especially common among modern Christians is the dualistic distinction between the personal and public roles of the Christian. In his personal role, it is argued, the Christian must always refuse to retaliate or kill. But the same person acting in the public role of judge or soldier rightly does both. Jesus then, they argue, was not forbidding capital punishment or war on the part of duly authorized Christian executioners and soldiers. He was merely forbidding private retaliation on the part of individuals who want to take the law into their own hands.

I disagree with this ethical dualism. I do not believe God has a double ethic. I am convinced that the only adequate explanation for the vigorous rejection of lethal violence by the early Christians is that Christ Himself commanded it. If so, Christians ought to forsake the diverse dualistic ethical systems developed since the fourth century and return to Jesus' teaching on nonretaliatory, suffering love, which is grounded in the cross.

That the cross is the ultimate demonstration that God deals with His enemies through suffering love receives its clearest theological expression in Saint Paul. "God shows his love for us in that while we were yet *sinners* Christ died for us . . . . While we were *enemies* we were reconciled to God by the death of his Son" (Rom. 5:8,10, italics added). Jesus' vicarious death on the cross for sinners is the foundation and deepest expression of Jesus' command to love one's enemies. As the substitutionary view of the atonement indicates, we are enemies in the double sense both that sinful persons are hostile to God and also that the just, holy Creator hates sin (Rom. 1:18).

Jesus' vicarious death for sinful enemies of God leads, I believe, to nonviolence. It was because the Incarnate One knew that God was loving and merciful even toward the worst of sinners that He associated with sinners, forgave their sins, and completed His messianic mission by dying for the sins of the world. And it was precisely the same understanding of God that prompted Him to command His followers to love their enemies. As God's children, we are to imitate the loving characteristics of our heavenly Father who mercifully showers His sun and rain on the just and the unjust. We are to imitate the Father who even takes the deserved punishment of our sinful rebellion upon Himself. That is why we are to love our enemies. The vicarious cross of Christ is the fullest expression of the character of God. The cross demonstrates that in His very essence God is self-sacrificial love. At the cross, God Himself suffers for sinners in the person of His Incarnate Son. Certainly we can never fathom all the mystery there. But it is precisely because the One hanging limp on the cross was the Word who became flesh that we are absolutely sure of two interrelated things: first, that a just God mercifully accepts us sinful enemies, and second, that He wants us to go and treat all our enemies in the same merciful, self-sacrificial way.

Since Jesus commanded His followers to love their enemies, and then died as the Incarnate Son to demonstrate that God reconciles His enemies by suffering love, any rejection of the nonviolent way in human relations seems to me to involve an incomplete doctrine of the atonement. If God in Christ reconciled His enemies by suffering servanthood, should not those who want to follow Christ faithfully also treat their enemies in the same way? The atonement was God's way of dealing with us as His enemies. Dare we refuse to imitate God's way in dealing with our enemies?

I have argued that I believe the teaching and cross of Christ lead to the total rejection of lethal violence. Does that mean that I advocate a passive acquiescence in the face of evil, including the ghastly evil of Soviet totalitarianism? Does that mean that we must unilaterally disarm? By no means. I vigorously reject that approach. I am ready to die to defend democratic freedom. But I am not willing to kill hundreds of millions of other people in that struggle for liberty and freedom.

I believe we should do two things. First, we should work very hard for bilateral and multilateral disarmament starting with a nuclear freeze. What do we do, however, if we cannot negotiate bilateral nuclear disarmament with the Soviets? Notice, please, that this is just as big a problem for many Just-War folk as for those committed to nonviolence. If, as many people in the Just-War tradition believe, that tradition leads to the rejection both of the use and the ongoing possession of nuclear weapons, then Just-War advocates also face the difficult question: How can we defend democracy without nuclear weapons?

I think there is an alternative to unilateral disarmament on the one hand and on the other the present madness that leads to global suicide. It is civilian-based defense. More and more scholars and military specialists are urging us to explore seriously the possibility of applying the nonviolent techniques of Gandhi and Martin Luther King to the task of national self-defense. We would have to decide as a nation that in, say, five to eight years, we would totally dismantle our nuclear and conventional weapons. In the intervening years we would spend billions of dollars to train the entire population in sophisticated techniques of nonviolent self-defense.

I cannot spell out here how this would work in detail. Dick Taylor and I have done that in the last section of our book *Nuclear Holocaust and Christian Hope.* There are hundreds of instances from past history where some form of nonviolent civilian-based defense has been used by societies. But it has almost always happened spontaneously with little prior planning. If a careful national, and even international, strategy of civilian-based defense were developed over a number of years, it would have even more possibility of success. Of course there is no guarantee that it would prevent terrible bloodshed, but then the way of the sword has not been terribly successful either.

If the American people somehow found the faith and courage to abandon lethal weapons in favor of civilian-based defense, we would almost certainly suffer. We would undoubtedly lose access to raw materials and international markets and our affluent standard of living would decline. We might very well experience a Soviet invasion. Resisting that invasion with love, prayer, and noncooperation would result in terrible suffering and many deaths. However, if hundreds of thousands of committed, praying Christians died in a massive nonviolent campaign of noncooperation with the Communist invaders, thus demonstrating that because of Christ's cross they wanted to suffer rather than commit global genocide, I predict that we would see the most rapid expansion of Christian faith that the world has ever known.

I am, of course, very aware of the fact that this proposal for civilian-based defense will not be adopted tomorrow by any one of the major political parties. In fact, I have little hope of it ever being adopted—or even of our avoiding nuclear holocaust, unless God's Holy Spirit sends a mighty revival sweeping across North America, Western Europe, and the Soviet Union. I want to beg you to pray for that peace revival.

In the past, great revivals have led to social movements that changed history. The Wesleyan revival led to Wilberforce's evangelical crusade to abolish the slave trade. The great revivals of the mid-nineteenth century led to a biblical, spirit-filled movement against slavery in our own land. Nothing less than the greatest revival in human history will save us from nuclear disaster.

Let us pray for a mighty revival that brings millions of sinners into a living personal relationship with Jesus Christ. Let us pray for a revival that restores millions of lukewarm church members. Let us pray that the Holy Spirit leads those transformed by revival to join the Prince of Peace in a worldwide crusade for the abolition of nuclear weapons. Let us pray for a peace revival in which people see that Jesus is the only way to peace and peace is the will of Jesus. Jesus means peace. Peace means Jesus.

Let us pray daily that God will spare us from nuclear war. As biblical Christians who know the power of Spirit-filled, intercessory prayer, let us have prayer groups in all our congregations praying for a peace revival that leads to nuclear disarmament. Let us have every Christian congregation in the United States form a prayer group interceding with God for the abolition of all nuclear weapons. Let us have all-night prayer chains pleading with God for a bilateral nuclear freeze. Let us have tens of millions of Christians all around the world constantly breathing the breath prayer to God, "Lord Jesus, please remove the mountain of nuclear weapons."

We face an ultimate choice in human history. The way of violence has led to ever escalating wars with ever more deadly weapons and ever larger numbers of dead. If we continue down that path, we will self-destruct.

There is an alternative. It is the way of the cross. It is a tough, hard path strewn with pain, crucifixion and hell. But it is probably the only way to avoid nuclear holocaust. And Jesus reminds us that the resurrection will surely follow.

Notes

1. Martin Hengel, *Victory Over Violence,* (London: SPCK, 1975), p. 71.
2. There are explicit quotations (Matt. 8:17; 12:17-21; Luke 22:37; John 12:38) and numerous allusions. See W. Zimmerli and J. Jeremias, *The Servant of God,* Studies in Biblical Theology, 2nd ser.: no. 20 (Naperville, IL: Alec R. Allenson, Inc., 1971).
3. John Piper, *Love Your Enemies,* Society for New Testament Studies: no. 38 (Cambridge: Cambridge University Press, 1979), pp. 21-48.
4. Eduard Schweizer, *The Good News According to Matthew,* (Atlanta: John Knox Press, 1975), p. 132.

Chapter Seven

Nonviolence as a Life-style
by Myron Augsburger

Our consideration of nonviolence as a life-style for Christians begins with the recognition that all of us have a certain amount of personal power. One of the questions we must ask ourselves is how we should use that power.

Lewis B. Smedes, in his book on 1 Corinthians 13, states that love is personal power used to help or enrich another individual. He describes servant love as personal power used to help a weaker person and collegial love as personal power used to help a colleague or a competitor.[1] I would like to underscore the statement that love is the use of personal power to help another. Jesus said that the Gentiles lorded over one another, but "it shall not be so among you" (Matt. 20:25,26). In contrast, Jesus described the role of the servant to mean that whatever power you have, you use it as a servant.

The Bible says that "though he was rich, yet for your sake he became poor" (2 Cor. 8:9). The classic passage on the Incarnation in Philippians 2 tells us that Jesus, "who, though he was in the form of God, did not count equality with God a thing to be grasped, but emptied himself, taking the form of a servant, being born in the likeness of men" (vv. 6,7).

I am suggesting that one cannot understand nonviolence as a life-style without coming to grips with the basic question of the use of power. We must not deny that we have power. When Esther and I moved to Washington, D.C., this struck me in a dramatic fashion. I had been at Eastern Mennonite College and Seminary for twenty-two years, fifteen years as president, and was known all over that small town of twenty thousand plus. I could walk into any store, buy something, sign my name, walk out, and pay them in thirty or sixty days. Then we moved to Washington, D.C., and they did not know Myron Augsburger from Adam. In the stores I had to pull out two I.D.'s for every check I wrote. I had power, but I had lost some of it. Power is not something that only the president or the Congress has, but power is something you and I have to deal with as well.

Dealing with power is a problem that is general in society. Several years ago I flew to Chicago from Princeton, where we were studying for a year. I walked through O'Hare Airport and out front to wait for a limousine to take me to the Oakbrook Sheraton. I had been invited to speak to the Oakbrook Executives' Club the next morning at a breakfast meeting. As I stood on the sidewalk, I overheard two men talking and discerned that they were going to the Oakbrook Sheraton also. I stepped over to them and said, "I believe you men are going to the Oakbrook Sheraton." They responded, "Yes." I replied, "I am as well. Why don't we team up, get a taxi, and split the cost three ways; it won't cost us any more and we won't have to wait." They agreed and we did.

We got in the taxi, the one man sitting in front beside the driver and the other man sitting in the back beside me. The two men chatted a little bit, and then the one next to me turned and asked, "Are you here for the agricultural equipment convention at the Sheraton?" I said, "No, I'm here to speak at the Oakbrook Executives' Club tomorrow morning." He asked, "What's that?" So I told him what I knew about it, that they bring a speaker in once a month to address some issue. Then he asked, "What's your topic?" I said, "Love, Power, and Freedom." And immediately he said, "They don't fit." I replied, "It depends on your definition. If you've got power and don't have love, what is going to keep power from being tyranny? Because power without love is going to be tyranny and then there's no freedom. But if you've got power and have love, then you can safeguard the freedom of the other individual and maximize his or her fulfillment." He sat there in silence for a moment and then he said, "Young man, if you could get that message across, you'd change the world."

This is one of the issues at stake when we take Jesus seriously. I believe that one of our problems is that many Christians have tried to write Jesus' teachings off as though irrelevant, or as though we cannot apply what He taught in our time.

There is a second issue involved here, and it has to do with the primacy of Kingdom theology and Kingdom ethics. By Kingdom I mean the rule of God in the disciples of Christ. This is not as Walter Rauschenbush put it in his theology for the social gospel, in which he said, "The Kingdom of God is society organized according to the will of God." No, I am referring to the Kingdom of God as expressed in the people of God, in the Church as it lives by the will of God. Wherever God is ruling, wherever Christ is ruling, there the Kingdom is happening.

Several summers ago, Jay Kesler, Ron Sider, Carl Henry and I were in the home of the late Frank Gaebelein, and he was telling us that he had been asked to write an article for *Christianity Today* on twenty-five years of the history of *CT* and of change in the church in that twenty-five years. He looked around the table and said, "One thing that has hit me is that twenty-five years ago we weren't talking about discipleship very much, we weren't talking about the meaning of the Kingdom, about Kingdom theology." He said, "We were afraid to talk about it lest people think we were going off on some liberal, social gospel movement. But," he said, "today we are talking about the Kingdom and about discipleship."

The importance of understanding the Kingdom of God is now emphasized in a very meaningful way in many evangelical circles. Once you take the Kingdom of Christ seriously, then you bring every earthly kingdom under its judgment. We have the responsibility to discern the meaning of loyalty to Christ over against the other loyalties to which we are called.

Such an issue as "render to Caesar the things that are Caesar's, and to God the things that are God's" (Luke 20:25) becomes very crucial for us. If we give God what is God's, it will not be difficult to give to Caesar the limited things that are Caesar's. There will not be that much which we are giving to Caesar, for loyalty to Caesar is not to interfere with the things of God. But we often turn this around the other way, and placing Caesar first we do not have much left to give to God!

The third thing I want to emphasize as a problem in evangelical churches is the relationship between ethics and grace. As my friend Bill Leslie from the LaSalle Street Church in Chicago puts it, "Something tragic happened to the American Christian Church when we moved away from salvation by faith to salvation by belief." Salvation by faith has to do with an identification with Jesus, a trust, a relationship. Salvation by belief puts the focus on believing certain concepts. Once we move in that direction, we have a problem as to how we bring in ethics, for you may begin feeling that you have emphasized works over against faith.

We should relate ethics to Christology in the same way that we relate salvation to Christology. We are saved in relating to Jesus and we behave in relation to Jesus. This is a perspective that I think the Christian Church needs to rediscover.

The question now becomes, who is the Jesus we are relating to? Is it the sweet Jesus of pietism? Is it the Jesus of neo-orthodoxy? Is it the Jesus of certain theologians or the Jesus of liberation theology? Or is it just the pietistic Jesus of much of evangelical thought, a private Jesus? Or is it the actual Jesus, who not only lived in history but is in history as a risen person, who is King of kings and Lord of lords?

My understanding of this Jesus is that He revealed the will of God in what He said, in what He did, and in what He was, all three. Most of us like to accept Jesus in what He did. He died on the cross for my sins, which is true. But He also revealed the will of God in what He said. For this same Jesus said that the only branch that bears fruit is the one that abides in the vine. "Apart from me you can do nothing" (John 15:5). He also said, "Love your enemies, . . . bless those who curse you" (Luke 6:27,28). Again He said, "Seek first his kingdom and his righteousness, and all these things shall be yours as well" (Matt. 6:33) as seren-dipitous.

He revealed the will of God in what He said as well as in what He did, but also in what He was. He modeled the one real person that we have ever seen in history. All the rest of us are perversions. We do not fully know what a real person is like except as we see a true person in Jesus.

When we understand that we have been created in the image of God, then we understand that redemption is not only a promise of forgiveness and an insurance policy that will guarantee that we will get to heaven when we die, but it is the restoration now of the *imago Dei*. Salvation is the re-creating of the true person that God intended us to be, the re-creating of the truly human.

The greatest affirmation of humanness the world has ever seen is incarnation of Jesus. In the Incarnation, God demonstrated that He could become human without being sinful. Redemption is the re-creating of the truly human.

What does it mean to be a truly human person? When Jesus was asked what was the first and great commandment, he said, "To love God" (see Matt. 22:37). I learned a definition of love a few years ago from a book entitled *Christianity and Existentialism*. The author defines love as the act in which one's life is intimately open to that of another. When I read that I said, "I can get hold of that. My life is open to Esther in a way it isn't open to anybody else in the world."

Jesus tells us to open our lives to God completely. We are to love God with our hearts, that is, open our affection to Him; with our minds, that is, to open our attitudes to Him; with our strength, to open our activity to Him; with our souls, open our ambition to Him. This interpretation of love makes clear how the second commandment is just like the first. Jesus said, "Love your neighbor as yourself" (Matt. 22:39). This means that once you open your life to God, you open it to what God is doing in your neighbor, be he your friend or your enemy. You cannot close anybody out.

This kind of love is costly. Nonviolence is simply the practice of love in relationship. Love is a proper participation with other persons whose commitments are not the same as ours, whose priorities are not the same as ours. Nonviolence means that we have a pattern of acting and behaving in society where the Christian knows that he is "in the world but not of the world," knows that "all who desire to live a godly life in Christ Jesus will be persecuted" (2 Tim. 3:12). Jesus said, "I have not come to bring peace, but a sword" (Matt. 10:34), by which He meant that He is the most divisive person in the world. Just as soon as you identify with Jesus, you run into resistance from every person that does not want to identify with Him. Persons will resent you because you are a constant reminder to them of Jesus.

We cannot live for Jesus and avoid what I am saying about the issue of nonviolent redemptive love in human relationships. Let me offer an affirmation that has become a very basic part of my theology. The affirmation is this: If love was possible without the gospel, we would need no gospel. If love was not possible by the gospel, then we have no gospel. That love is possible by the gospel is what Christian discipleship is all about! Love is possible by the gospel, because God has spread love in our hearts by the Holy Spirit. In 1 John 4:8 it says, "He that loveth not knoweth not God; for God is love" *(KJV)*.

The central biblical passage for our reflection on nonviolence as a life-style comes from Luke 6:27-36:

> But I say to you that hear, Love your enemies, do good to those who hate you, bless those who curse you, pray for those who abuse you. To him who strikes you on the cheek, offer the other also; and from him who takes away your cloak do not withhold your coat as well. Give to every one who begs from you; and of him who takes away your goods do not ask them again. And as you wish that men would do to you, do so to them. If you love

those who love you, what credit is that to you? For even sinners love those who love them. And if you do good to those who do good to you, what credit is that to you? For even sinners do the same. And if you lend to those from whom you hope to receive, what credit is that to you? Even sinners lend to sinners, to receive as much again. But love your enemies, and do good, and lend, expecting nothing in return; and your reward will be great, and you will be the sons of the Most High; for he is kind to the ungrateful and the selfish. Be merciful, even as your Father is merciful.

There are three things I want to lift out of this passage, and in my judgment they interpret what Jesus is saying, and they are the groundwork for my beliefs concerning a nonviolent life-style.

The three points are these: first, love elevates others above yourself; second, love elevates persons above the material; and third, love elevates behavior above bargaining.

In the first place, love elevates others above yourself. When Jesus says, "Love your enemies," He calls us to be concerned about the person, not about what he or she is doing to us. We pray for those who abuse us. We bless those who curse us. This brings a positive influence into the lives of others. This is not a passivism. There is a difference between being a pacifist and being passive. I do not like the word pacifist as well as the term nonresistance, although I am a committed pacifist. I do not know any better way to identify myself with the way we use language today. But it is an inadequate word. It is not a New Testament word. But for the sake of communication, I do identify as a pacifist. My commitment to Jesus calls me to peace and to justice and to the simple life, in that order. But Jesus is first. I am first of all committed to Jesus, not to the simple life.

A nonviolent life-style involves an active dimension of love, the active practice of love. When love elevates others above yourself it means that if somebody smites you on one cheek, you turn the other to him. I submit to you that this is the Christian's strategy of operation. This is in no way a surrender. The only free person in the world is the one who turns the other cheek. The only free person in the world is the nonconformist.

When Jesus said you should turn the other cheek, He was giving us a stance of operation in which we are saying, I am free to have my behavior toward you determined by another standard, another loyalty, another set of principles, than to have my behavior toward you determined by the way you have treated me.

That is freedom. Elevating another above yourself allows you freedom to make the decisions concerning how you will act, react, and interact with that person. Martin Luther King, Jr., in his book *Stride Toward Freedom*, writes: "Not only do we avoid violence of deed but violence of spirit." That is what I am talking about if love is an attitude of the heart, and that is not easy, especially when it means loving your enemy.

One famous rabbinical scholar said that you can find all of the teachings of the Sermon on the Mount in the Torah except one statement: love your enemies. All of the rest is there, he says. The most unique thing about the ethics of Jesus is to love our enemies.

The second point: love elevates persons above the material. If somebody takes your coat, you are to give him your cloak or your vest also. "Give to him who begs from you, and do not refuse him who would borrow from you"

(Matt. 5:42). I have heard persons say that this is impossible in our kind of society. On the other hand, I would say that if you understand the spirit of the passage, its basic intent, then it is not only possible in our society but it is the only way to overcome the problems we have in a competitive economy that locks the "haves" into one level and the "have-nots" into another. Mark Hatfield has said that for the last twenty-five years, 25 percent of the American people live on 75 percent of its resources, and 75 percent of the American people live on 25 percent of its resources. You know that 7 percent of the world's population lives on 50 percent of the global resources that are available. In this kind of world, we need to understand what it means to "give to him who begs from you."

My brother-in-law has been a missionary in India for thirty-some years, and has supervised grain distribution during the famine in Bahir. During the whole time of the famine, the missionaries called a moratorium on accepting any converts to Christianity because they knew that if they baptized people the Hindus would say, "They are wheat Christians. You bought them." So they did not baptize for the whole period of the famine. When it was over, a lot of people came and said, "We want to know about Christ because there was something different about the way you served us." Many became Christians and came into the church.

It is possible to have an authentic compassion that cares about helping people in the name of Jesus without concern for what you are going to get out of it. John Perkins says, "You don't have to give people dignity. God has already given them that. Just recognize it."

To elevate persons above the material, however, has other implications. We are a part of a society which has operated for years by relating property and life, and to take the life of persons who are violating property rights has been an acceptable thing. You can shoot a man for robbing your store.

There are dimensions here that we have to answer. Why do we put property so high in comparison to the value of human life? Property is to be used for the good of people. As someone said, "The world is made for man, not man for the world." Money is to be used, and to be used for the well-being of people. This is the principle that is coming through in Jesus' teachings.

The third point: love elevates behavior above bargaining. If you only respond on the basis of what you are getting back, you are behaving just like any other sinner, Jesus says. If you loan money at the highest interest rates, that is no different than what people can get elsewhere from anyone else.

We do not have to live that way. Let me illustrate this point. I know a very successful medical doctor who has served at the Mayo Clinic. He graduated from Eastern Mennonite College in pre-med and went on through medical school. He was a rather poor boy who could not afford to go to college, but an older man that I knew as a friend financed his way through school. The man told him, "When you are a successful medical doctor, help somebody else through school just as I'm helping you. It's a loan, but I don't want it back. The money is God's." This is what I am talking about.

In this passage Jesus also says we should not only have people over to dinner that are going to have us back. We should not just loan on the basis of what we are going to receive. "You, therefore, must be perfect, as your heavenly Father is perfect" (Matt. 5:48). (In Luke 6:36, the same thought is communicated in a different way—"Be merciful, even as your Father is merciful.") As God is perfect in love for all alike, so we are to be perfect without respect of persons.

Nonviolence as a life-style is not passivism; it is active, aggressive involvement for the well-being of our fellow-man. Some people argue, "Well, if everybody took your position, what would happen? Suppose the government of the U.S. took this position, wouldn't it be overrun by evil?"

This position is for the disciples of Christ, for His Church. If Christians lived in this way society would be better. We could change the world if we had thousands of Christians who would be willing to permeate countries with the gospel, not to go there in a preacher pattern but to flesh out faith by a Christian presence in loving and compassionate service. We could do more by love to change the relationship between us and other persons of the world than guns and bombs and tanks can ever do.

Back in 1964 Esther and I were in India for mission conventions. For a break we were going from Delhi down to Agra to see the Taj Mahal. We got on a bus for the ride down, and there was a middle-aged American couple on the bus, and, since we were expatriates also, we struck up a conversation. I had never heard a man use such vile, negative language about America and her policies, and yet he was working for the U.S. State Department. He had been in Afghanistan for sixteen years with the U.S. State Department. He said, "We are so dumb. We are outfoxed by the Russians again and again. They come into Afghanistan and build reservoirs, tanks for water, while the Americans come in with a lot of money and build airports and lay macadam strips, and the sand blows the buildings full. Every morning when the Afghan women go to the tank to get their water for their family they bless the Russians, and they look over at those airport facilities and curse the Americans."

What he was saying twenty years ago has born fruit in the past several years. We shouldn't put so much confidence in our bigness and our power. It seems that we have got to be number one, that we have got to win. For many, life is not a matter of being our brother's brother.

I submit to you that nonviolence as a life-style can be carried out on an international basis. The Christian Church of which we are a part is global, transnational, and transcultural. Christian people should begin doing the things we ought to do together across national lines, and quit acting as though the issues that we are facing will all have to be answered between Washington and Moscow. We should begin belting the globe with relationships across national lines, in order to make it a lot easier for governments to negotiate their differences. The Christian community in prayer and sharing does have the tremendous possibility of changing the direction of the nations if we will lock arms with Christian people around the world. Nonviolence is what Jesus taught, did, and was. And nonviolence works, both on a personal level and on an international level. This is clearly a New Testament message.

Note
1. Lewis B. Smedes, *Love Within Limits*, (Grand Rapids: Wm. B. Eerdmans Publishing Co., 1978).

Chapter Eight

A Peace Lover's Pilgrimage
by Vernon C. Grounds

Autobiography fascinates me. I find few things more engrossing than the chronicle of some fellow-pilgrim's life journey, like Augustine's *Confessions* or C.S. Lewis's *Surprised by Joy*. Augustine and Lewis were, of course, extraordinary human beings, but in my opinion the histories of ordinary human beings are often scarcely less interesting. So I hope that what I relate concerning one segment of my own odyssey may prove of some encouragement to other travelers through space-time. I hope it will be of value especially to my co-believers who are trying to keep in mind and work out in practice our Lord's promise which is an implied command, "Blessed are the peacemakers."

How do convictions take root and grow? What are the influences that conspire to forge stubborn beliefs? How obedient have we been to the insights which God has providentially granted us? I delve down into those vast chambers of memory which so intrigued Augustine, and I emerge with a twofold reaction—on the one hand, gratitude; on the other, humility.

I was born in Jersey City, New Jersey, on July 19, 1914, the third child of middle-class parents. A bit of rapid arithmetic therefore supplies the information that I am a member of the geriatric set, an earthling who now may apply personally the three-score-and-ten-year milestone which the psalmist declares to be the average existence-span of humankind. Making my planetary debut at the outset of the First World War, I have lived through one of history's most turbulent eras, an epoch of unprecedented change, catastrophe and crisis. Yet as a citizen of the United States of America, my own experiences have been placid and tranquil, largely exempt from pain and tragedy. I do not know except imaginatively—with imagination sharpened by travel overseas—the hunger, injustice, violence, suffering, and despair which are the lot of most people.

Thus when I speak about peacemaking, I sense keenly that I am in the position of a theoretician, neither one of war's participants nor one of its victims. I have never been caught up in armed conflict. I have never lived under a dictatorship where terror and torture fill life with anxiety and dread. I have never wandered homeless with my family as a refugee. Reflecting, then, on the contrast between myself and millions of my contemporaries, I quote subvocally those pride-pulverizing lines:

> The toad beneath the harrow knows
>   Exactly where each tooth-point goes;
> The butterfly upon the road
>   Preaches contentment to the toad.

In attempting to trace out the sources of my attitude towards war and peace, I have wondered if we are born with certain predispositions. Gilbert and Sullivan may have been near the truth when in their operetta *Iolanthe* they have a character sing—and of course the lines must be made to rhyme:

> I often think it's comical
> How nature always does contrive
> That every boy and every gal,
> That's born into the world alive,
> Is either a little Liberal,
> Or else a little Conservative!

Perhaps I was born with certain convictional predispositions. Inheritor of a fallen nature with a proclivity towards aggressive egocentricity, I seemed nevertheless to have an innate antipathy towards violence and bloodshed. From earliest on, at any rate, my whole being recoiled with utmost repugnance from the infliction of pain on the smallest of sentient creatures.

I have a vivid recollection of standing at the age of four in the midst of a very noisy crowd on the boulevard in Jersey City gazing at an effigy of Kaiser Wilhelm dangling high above the street. That was at the end of World War I in 1918. What my feelings may have been I cannot recall, other than bewilderment that everybody seemed to hate the man whose image was hanging in midair.

Later, as a boy, whatever may have been my convictional predispositions, I played soldier with my friends day after day. What fierce battles we fought, all of them fortunately with bloodless casualties and corpses immediately resurrected!

No matter how I ransack my memory, I cannot clearly

remember whether anybody in my family or school or even church said much about war. I suspect, though, that I must have overheard adult conversation regarding the horrors of the recently-ended conflict between Germany and the Allies.

I began to read and I read avidly, maybe even a little precociously. I also began to hear broadcasts on our crystal set, a primitive type of radio which only members of the geriatric age group will recall. Some of my friends and I had serious discussions concerning heavy issues like politics, including the rightness and wrongness of killing state-certified enemies. While the thoughts of youth, as the poet puts it, are long, long thoughts, it must not be imagined that we juveniles were budding philosophers! But moving into early adolescence and entering high school, we were becoming aware that all the flag waving and patriotic rhetoric merely camouflaged the agony and insanity of international slaughter. Besides that, we were children of the Great Depression who realized that democratic governments no less than dictatorial regimes can be woefully shortsighted and mistaken in the actions they take or fail to take.

How during those formative years I gradually became an ardent idealist is impossible for me to explain. I simply know that by the time I entered Rutgers University in 1933, I had developed an invincible prejudice against killing in any form. That prejudice, no doubt fostered by my reading and reflection, was not logically reasoned out. Neither was it biblically grounded. All I know is that as a college freshman I refused to take the required ROTC (Reserve Officers' Training Corps) training on the ground of conscientious objection. God alone is privy to what had gone on in the depths of my mind and heart to bring me to that decision. I am at a loss to explain precisely why I made it. My basic motivation, I surmise, was humanitarian. But somehow or other that anti-war mindset had crystalized.

My roommate at Rutgers, arbitrarily assigned to live with me, was C. Kilmer Myers, who later, much later, succeeded James Pike as the Episcopal bishop of Northern California. Strange the divergence of pathways on our pilgrimages! Kim became an Episcopal bishop; I became president of the Conservative Baptist Theological Seminary. Divergent pathways indeed! Both of us, however, were conscientious objectors and campus liberals. In fact, some of my evangelical brothers and sisters are still shocked to learn that I, together with Kim and a few other quasi-radicals, organized the Student Strike Against War and Fascism there at Rutgers in the spring of 1934. It is difficult for my friends to picture me, now a white-haired image of ecclesiastical respectability, riding around the campus in a sound-truck urging students to leave their classes and join a mass rally of passionate protest. We were protesting because Europe was once again heading for a blood bath. We resonated with Robert Louis Stevenson who, when he learned about the outbreak of the first World War, lay on the ground and writhed in anguish. As a matter of fact, I contributed a poem to the university's literary magazine, my copy of which I can nowhere locate. Laurence Stallings had published a book entitled *The First World War: A Photographic History.* As in horror I pondered its pages, I felt constrained in my poeticized "Review" to ask about a butchered human being:

Was this monstrosity a man,
The known kin of Jehovah's clan?

Then, after several additional stanzas which cannot be exhumed from the graveyard of memory, I concluded with this exclamation:

Oh idiotic world self-cursed,
Why do you strive to justify
The implications of the First?

As a college student I shuddered to think that the second World War might break out. It did. Yes, alas, it did; a war more terrible, far more terrible, than the first.

At this juncture I must mention a life-changing event which occurred during the summer between my freshman and sophomore years. Though I had been reared in the church and had enrolled at Rutgers University as a pre-ministerial student, I had never experienced a personal relationship with Jesus Christ as my Saviour and Lord. Indeed, immersed in philosophy, history, and literature, I had lost all faith in any supernaturalism—not an uncommon college experience. The wavering beliefs I had brought to the university were eroded by the impact of my studies. So I had made up my mind to abandon mythological religion, resign from my church, and join the American Humanist Society. God in His grace intervened, however, and early in June, shortly after I returned home, I encountered the living Christ.

Consequently, that fall I went back to Rutgers and continued my preparation for the pastoral ministry, but I did so with a sense of commitment and mission I had never previously possessed. The Bible now took on exciting relevance as I read it and sought stumblingly to live under its authority. As a sequel to my conversion, I spent more and more time with friends who were enthusiastic fundamentalists and ecclesiastical separatists. Of one thing I was sure: to keep my life-transforming faith in Jesus Christ it was evidently imperative that I remain in fellowship with the biblicists who had introduced me to the Saviour. Not surprisingly, therefore, in 1937 I enrolled at the newly organized Faith Theological Seminary in Wilmington, Delaware, a seminary which under the leadership of Carl McIntire had broken away from Westminster Theological Seminary, and Westminster only a few years before had broken away from Princeton Theological Seminary. Thus I was swept up into right-wing evangelicalism. While at Faith and after graduating from that seminary, I pastored a nondenominational congregation in Paterson, New Jersey, a congregation which identified itself with the Independent Fundamental Churches of America.

During my years in the pastorate—they were also years of doctrinal study—I carried on a debate with myself about the anti-war stance I had taken. You see, it was and is virtually axiomatic within the orbit of separatistic fundamentalism that no biblicist can be a pacifist. Yes, members of some traditionally nonresistant denominations like the Church of the Brethren are both biblicists and pacifists, but they must be viewed as paradoxical aberrations. No pacifism and scripturally-oriented Christianity are irreconcilable. You can be a misguided pacifist or you can be an authentic Christian, but you cannot be both.

For one thing, the argument goes, pacifism equals liberalism. Certainly! How can you accept as an inerrant revelation the Old Testament with its war-commanding, genocide-sanctioning God and at the same time be a pacifist? For a second thing, pacifism equals postmillennialism: the heretical *(sic)* teaching that eventually the world will be thoroughly evangelized, even Christianized, the Kingdom of God established by human effort; and then, only then, after a man-made millennium of peace and righteousness, Christ will return. Postmillennialism entails a denial of dispensational premillennialism, the theological system which dominated and still dominates American evangelicalism. For a third thing, pacifism equals utopianism, a sentimental optimism which is blind to original sin and human depravity; it refuses to face the brutal realities of history; it goes hand in hand with a starry-eyed internationalism that is willing to sell patriotism down the river; it is a gullible naiveté which imagines that diabolical evils like Nazism and communism can be stopped by spineless appeasement *a la* Chamberlain at Munich rather than by military might. Such, in brief, were some of the assumptions and arguments which persuaded my fellow biblicists—and when articulated with exegetical and logical sophistication challenged my own nonresistant position—that no Christian living under the authority of God's Word can be a pacifist.

No wonder, then, that the Just-War principles became more persuasive when neo-pagan Nazism ruthlessly overran Europe. No wonder, either, that when the Japanese attack on Pearl Harbor catapulted our country into the conflict, I and many others like myself were inwardly torn. Our nonresistant convictions had to be rethought and restudied. Reinhold Niebuhr, a penetrating ethicist and early-on a staunch pacifist, had done just that. Compelled, he said, by the grim irrationality and demonic savagery of Adolf Hitler's merciless conquest of nearly all Europe, he had made an about-face. A convert to Christian realism, he had become its most persuasive advocate, attacking the fatuous illusions and errors of pacifism. And indeed if ever there seemed to be a war which could be justified by the principles of Christian realism, this was it.

Ah, how troubled some of us were, biblicists like myself, who aspired to follow the Prince of Peace! Had we been tragically mistaken in our understanding of Scripture? Were we sincerely mistaken in our nonresistant beliefs—sincere yet wrong, terribly wrong, because (and today the same indictment is leveled against advocates of a nuclear freeze) a peace-loving nation without a will to arm and fight becomes a sitting duck for a totalitarian predator? How troubled we were by the indiscriminate bombing of nonmilitary targets, a strategy which violated the Just-War principles Christians had historically espoused! How troubled we were when our country incinerated Hiroshima and Nagasaki with a ghastly weapon never before available, the A-bomb which unleashed nature's ultimate powers of destruction! How troubled we were after World War II ended to watch the outbreak of war after war in several of which our own nation fought, notably the struggle in Viet Nam! How troubled we were and are by the improvement and proliferation of nuclear weaponry! How troubled we were and are by Washington's refusal to abandon a first-strike policy or to push resolutely towards a realistic arms control!

Troubled, ambivalent, torn by uncertainty, I carried on my ministry and continued my doctoral program, serving on the side as a professor at King's College. In 1945 I became dean of Baptist Bible Seminary in Johnson City, New York, a school sponsored by the General Association of Regular Baptists. In 1951, I joined the faculty of the Conservative Baptist Seminary in Denver, where I am still teaching.

As professor of ethics I offered annually a required course on "The Contemporary World and the Christian Task." This, together with other responsibilities, forced me to grapple with the war issue not only philosophically but biblically. I prayerfully studied and restudied Scripture. I likewise read books that challenged me, clarified my mind, and brought me out of ambivalence into a renewed and re-crystalized anti-war, pro-peace mindset. What books? This is not the place for a detailed bibliography. Suffice it to say that I was immensely helped by, among others, C. H. C. McGreggor, Culbert Rutenber, John Ferguson, Jacques Ellul, John Yoder, and Gordon Zahn. Let me pause, however, to pay my tribute to Franz Jüggerstatter, the solitary witness about whom I learned from

Gordon Zahn, a solitary witness whose heroism jolted my conscience.

Born in the little town of Saint Radeguend, Austria, Franz lived there with his wife and three daughters, serving as the very devout sexton of his Roman Catholic church. In Saint Radeguend he no doubt would have eventually died except for his tenacious integrity, rooted in a profound faith.

A simple man with no training in theology or ethics, Franz underwent a transforming experience when at the age of twenty-nine he married and, with his wife, made a pilgrimage to Rome. From then on he was a dedicated Christian—a bit fanatical, some of his neighbors thought—singing as he did his daily chores and zealously seeking to maintain a constant piety in all he was and did. Then came Hitler's annexation of Austria.

Persuaded that the policies of the Third Reich were iniquitous, Franz was the only person in all his village who in the rigged plebicite had the courage to vote *Nein*. He was the only person in all his village who openly criticized the Nazis. He was the only man who refused to be conscripted for military service under Hitler. That refusal, he knew, might mean death. He refused nevertheless. Pressure, irresistible pressure, one might imagine, was brought to bear upon him. He still refused. Friends, neighbors, priests and prelates, a lawyer who admired him, members of his own family, pleaded and argued. Why not compromise? Why not serve in a non-combatant capacity? Why throw your life away in a futile sacrifice that will not stop the seemingly invincible *Wehrmacht*? Why stand alone even against the official position of the church? Why arrogantly trust your own conscience as if it were infallible? Nothing moved Franz. He would not in the slightest degree sanction or support the destructive forces of evil.

Shipped to Berlin, he was imprisoned there. On the

table in his cell lay the document which needed only his scribbled signature to stave off death. Steadfastly refusing to compromise, Franz spent his days and nights in prayer and worship, writing letters to his family and statements of his belief. While not literary masterpieces, they are indisputably moving testimonies to a faith that made an ordinary man a hero. Calm, unafraid to the end, he was beheaded on August 9, 1943.

Jüggerstatter's heroic fidelity, together with the example of other unsung disciples who courageously followed the Prince of Peace, forced me to face my own vacillation. In the end, though, it was my study of Scripture, illuminated by the insights of a host of scholars, which brought me to the place where I am now in my pilgrimage. And where is that? As a Christian who takes the Bible as his allsufficient rule of faith and practice, I am convinced that I must hold to a nonresistant position. In the name of Jesus my Saviour and Lord I must do more than hate and deplore war. I must stand against it absolutely and adamantly as a blatant and ghastly denial of all that the gospel proclaims and all that obedient discipleship demands.

As my own thinking has clarified and crystalized, I have tried to bear my witness chiefly within my evangelical orbit. I have therefore participated in conferences, seminars, and rallies, lectured at colleges, preached in churches and written articles and even a book trying to share my concern. That book, *Revolution and the Christian Faith,* was published in 1971. In it I examined the case for resorting to violence as a last-ditch effort of overthrowing oppressive tyranny and securing at least a minimal measure of food, freedom, and fulfillment for downtrodden people. I inquired whether a Just Revolution might be possible on the analogy of a Just War. My conclusion, heavily influenced by Jacques Ellul's analysis of violence, was negative.

In 1981, aroused and shaken by Jonathan Schell's *The Fate of the Earth,* I joined with my fellow Baptist, Senator Mark O. Hatfield of Oregon, in urging a nuclear freeze.

I have done and am doing what I can (though I must confess not all that I might be doing) because of my concern as an Evangelical about the unconcern which, in my judgment, prevails by and large among our biblically-oriented American churches. The matter which concerns me is an indifference to peacemaking. Our churches are laudably preoccupied with evangelism, personal piety, family relationships and in-group activities. They are engaged in praiseworthy battles against abortion, pornography, crime, family breakdown, alcoholism and the drug menace. But with noteable exceptions they are not equally concerned about economic justice, racial prejudice, the ecological hazard, and the unthinkable menace of a nuclear war. Indeed, I am deeply concerned because many of my fellow Evangelicals are hostile towards peacemaking. They allege that it is both unbiblical and futile; they sometimes insinuate that concern for peace is very liable to be Communist inspired.

On the other hand, there is a concern within many of our churches which causes me concern, a vigorous espousal by brothers and sisters whose sincerity I in no wise impugn. They are concerned that our country vastly increase its military muscle in order that we Americans can keep Soviet Russia from, as they perceive the danger, dominating our globe. That sabre-rattling, bomb-brandishing approach concerns me! I fear the America, as it becomes militarily powerful (and potentially a radioactive wasteland!), will continue to proudly boast, "We're Number One, and you bad guys had better watch your step." As I prayerfully imagine some possible scenarios of humanity's future, I am concerned that my grandchild and children everywhere be saved from a nuclear holocaust.

Thus as my career and my life are in their sunset phase, I am giving myself increasingly to what I consider the top priority moral issue of our time. How can nations which profess value of personhood continue to pursue policies which will result in a war guaranteed to annihilate millions upon millions of human beings, a war which will abandon all the time-honored principles of combat to which Christians have held, a war which will make vast areas of our world, if not the entire globe, a man-engineered Armageddon?

I am doing my limited best to articulate the Christian's role of peacemaker as I have come to understand it. This is a multi-dimensional task which includes peace between God and man through faith in the reconciling Saviour. It includes, too, peace of heart and soul as a fruit of the Holy Spirit in one's own experience. It includes, as well, peace on every level of relationship—peace in marriages, families, churches, businesses and industries. It must therefore include peace among the nations of the world. My concern and my conviction have been forged biblically and hence Christomorphically. If my life, my discipleship, my witness are to be shaped in keeping with the Jesus pattern, the *morphe* of Christ, I have no option but to give myself to the multidimensional task of peacemaking.

Let me conclude by spelling out my position in a series of suggestions which I have labelled "Strategies for Soldiers of Shalom."

"Blessed are the peacemakers." If we are to experience this beatitude which is a promise that implies a mandate, we must do more than extol peace as a Christian ideal—an ideal which is allegedly unattainable in our fallen world. We must take with complete seriousness the military language of the New Testament. We must be soldiers of our Lord Jesus, aggressively battling the destructive forces of evil. We must be battling for peace, using the arms which the Apostle Paul specifies in 2 Corinthians 10:4,5.

Here, then, are some principles which may help us implement our Lord's peacemaking mandate:

1. Unambiguously denounce and renounce war.

2. Pray! Pray daily and specifically, remembering not only 2 Corinthians 10:3-5, but also 1 Timothy 2:1-5 and Ephesians 6:1-10.

3. Keep informed regarding the development of international and national affairs: be concerned about the world, not just the Church.

4. Study and ponder biblical ethics.

5. Critically examine traditional and prevalent viewpoints and doctrines with respect to military policy—e.g. the Just-War theory, nuclear deterrence, the pacifist option.

6. Recognize that Christians, while grateful citizens of a particular country, belong to a kingdom which is global. Refuse to be an uncritical nationalist or an idolatrous American.

7. Support the historical right of dissent.

8. Obey the New Testament demand for Christian nonconformity.

9. Recognize that obedience to our Lord Jesus is the master-criterion of discipleship, not political effectiveness nor pragmatic success.

10. Use whatever political and propaganda resources are available to oppose those forces, ideologies, and institutions which foster an anti-peace mindset and a pro-war mentality.

11. Stress the interconnectedness of justice and peace. Battle injustice insofar as that is possible.

12. Collaborate with all peace-lovers in peacemaking, regardless of theological and ideological differences but within the limits imposed by Scripture and conscience.

13. Seek to be an agent of *shalom* in all personal relationships.

14. Hold steadily in view Romans 14:5.

15. Entertain no utopian illusions with respect to a permanently warless world until the King personally establishes His Kingdom. Believe that God wills *shalom* here and now.

Chapter Nine

Responding Faithfully as Followers of Jesus Christ in a Nuclear Age

by Mark O. Hatfield

I was serving in the United States Navy in the Pacific in September of 1945 when orders to survey the bombed city of Hiroshima came. The experience made an indelible impression on my mind. Most of my thinking, views, ideas, and attitudes are at least partly due to my experiences, background, heritage, and environment. On that particular day, all the bodies had not yet been removed from the rubble; all of our human senses were assaulted by the utter and total indiscriminate devastation caused by the dropping of one bomb—a very primitive bomb in comparison to what we now have in our arsenals. We saw nothing but destruction in every direction. The smell of the decomposition of human flesh and the silence that beset the city were overwhelming.

The United States arsenal is now equivalent to one

million Hiroshima bombs. The Soviet Union also has an arsenal equivalent to one million Hiroshima bombs. E.B. White wrote that the bombing of Hiroshima was an example of the "limitless power of the victor. The quest for the substitute for God ended suddenly. The substitute turned up and who do you suppose it was. It was man himself stealing God's stuff." We are the robbers of God's stuff, and it has not brought us prosperity. It has not brought us spiritual renaissance. It has not brought us security. It has not brought us peace. It has not created reconciliation. Rather, our robbery has foreordained the apocalypse.

A military man who witnessed the first detonation of atomic weapons at Alamagordo, New Mexico, said, "There was a rushing of the wind, there was a deathly silence, and then the detonation." And he said, "It almost seemed blasphemous, for we had released power heretofore reserved to the Almighty"—another way of stating the case that indeed with the opening of the atomic era and the nuclear age came man's power to destroy God's very creation. For humankind to stand shaking his fist in the heavens and saying in effect, "I not only have the capability, but I will even risk the potential destruction of creation" is the ultimate blasphemy, the ultimate obscenity.

How do we, as Kingdom people, respond to this tremendous power that has been released upon the earth and upon all life? Before us is the hubris of politicians and bureaucrats and experts with their terrible notion that this is but a process, a technique, a skill, and a science devoid of any human or spiritual dimension. Faced by this mindset, we ascribe an idolatrous power and ultimacy to nuclear weapons. This deepens our dependence upon them to the point at which they have become the substitute for God. Nuclear weapons have become our god. We have been victimized by our own discoveries and techniques because they are void of spiritual dimension. A sense of futility and an increase in our feelings of inevitable disaster—not by design but by accident—have overwhelmed us. This nonchalant approach to weapons is so tragic that we treat it in our budgetary process as we would treat an educational program—or a health program—or as we would treat a commodity such as wheat or gold. It has become just another program in the budgetary process. It is just another product to be funded by your taxes and developed by this country's tremendous resources.

But listen to that crusty, cantankerous Admiral Hyman Rickover. In his retirement speech he said, "The lessons of history are simple. When a war starts, every nation will ultimately use whatever weapon has been available. That is a lesson learned time and time again. Therefore we must expect, if another war—a serious war—breaks out we will use nuclear energy in some or all forms. That's due to the imperfection of human beings." Admiral Rickover realizes the probability of nuclear extinction and contends that weapons are not neutral, but rather introduce a compelling temptation for human beings to use them when they possess them.

I would like to share something beyond the superficial question usually posed when one talks about nuclear arms and the role of the Christian attempting to follow as a pilgrim in the Kingdom. Before us is not a question of pacifism or rational preparation, as it is so often posed. Rather, the question came from the mind of a five-star general, Dwight David Eisenhower, when he said, "What can the world or any nation in it hope for if no turning is found on this dread road? This is not a way of life at all. It is humanity hanging from a cross of iron." Whatever our political persuasion, whatever our religious conviction, we must recognize that humanity is presented with more than a question between pacifism or unilateral disarmament on one hand and wise and prudent preparation on the other hand. Such a choice implies that we are presently defenseless to our marching adversaries. In fact, our current stockpile today has a multiple overkill.

In other words: The United States has twenty-one nuclear submarines, two of which have the firepower to destroy every major Russian city; the Navy wants to build fifteen more. How many more? How much is sufficient? In building and adding to the nuclear arsenal someone once said, we simply make the rubble bounce. Yet we are programming one trillion seven hundred billion dollars of your tax money in the next five years for armaments. We must ask ourselves the question, What has been the cost— morally, spiritually, and to some the most important aspect of national security, economically? What price have we paid?

So you will understand my personal context of views, let me make a very clear statement from the outset. I believe what we are doing and what we have done is wrong, WRONG, *WRONG*. In theological terms, it is sin—s-i-n—to close this nation's eyes to the human cost of our supremely reckless course.

More people on this globe have died from starvation in the last five years than in the last one hundred and fifty years of war. That's part of the human cost. Consider these trade-offs. One half of the money we as a world bent on armament spend in half a day could eradicate malaria, one of the most debilitating of all diseases and part of the disease of war, from the face of the earth. The amount of money the world spends in two days on arms is more than the United Nations spends in an entire year through all of its programs to relieve human suffering. The cost of one modern tank could build a thousand classrooms to help educate thirty thousand children to help attack ignorance and illiteracy, another part of the disease of war. The cost of one jet fighter airplane could build forty thousand village pharmacies to bring elementary health care to people in the Third and Fourth World who never receive it. The money required to feed all of the poor of the world, to give them clean water, to give them an education, to give them access to health facilities and support, to give them decent housing for an entire year is equivalent to what all nations spend in two weeks on the arms race.

What then is the accountability of the Kingdom people? We live in a world of both corporate sin and personal sin. Sometimes, even in churches, we do not like to hear the subject of sin discussed. Dr. Karl Menninger, one of the great psychiatrists, wrote *Whatever Happened to Sin?* for just that reason. We have become too sophisticated to talk about sin. And yet sin is real. As we acquiesce by our absence of voice or by our supportive voice to national policies, we are committing corporate sin for which we will stand accountable to God. We are committing sin when we permit the continuation of policies that deny the bare necessity of existence to human life while we waste and squander our resources, continually escalating our resource expenditures into life-destroying endeavors.

We are ignoring the causes of war. We are ignoring the causes of violence. We are ignoring the injustices that pervade the universe. Like the sleeping, wealthy church at Sardis described by Saint John in the book of Revelation, we trust that we are impregnable because of our economic security and wealth, much like the ancient city of Sardis with its hilltop fortress. When Cyrus the Great overran that ancient city, it was lost because the people of Sardis had assumed their security and ignored their vulnerability. John the Revelator said, "Awake, and strengthen what remains and is on the point of death, for I have not found your works perfect in the sight of my God. . . . If you will not awake, I will come like a thief, and you will not know at what hour I will come upon you" (Rev. 3:2,3).

We should heed the warning of the church at Sardis. In many ways we, as the Christian institution today, are wealthy in economic terms. We have magnificent buildings. We even have endowments. Yet is that the source of our strength? Is that really our security?

Today, many of us view the current hard-line approach to the Soviet Union with ambivalence. We view our own nation's position with ambivalence. Many of us fear nuclear confrontation but tend to favor strong signals aimed at discouraging the Kremlin from brutal adventurism. I, too, favor effective signals and effective action. But we are not sending effective signals. Our deeds are not complete. This macho facade only disguises ineptitude and profound recklessness on both sides. By the end of the century, sixty nations of the world will be capable of developing nuclear weaponry. And those who are madly pursuing this capability, like Colonel Khadafy of Libya, and General Zia of Pakistan, and India and others, are leaders of desperate, unstable nations oftentimes without a subsistence agriculture base to feed their own people. We know from past history that desperate people do desperate things, and I am only surprised that we have not already found ourselves victims of nuclear blackmail.

Instead of trying to extinguish this brush fire, we are throwing fuel on the flames of instability and self-destruction by becoming the largest arms peddler in the world. We are even peddlers of materials that can be used in developing nuclear weaponry. Today we fully arm any nation in the Third and Fourth World which claims it does not like the Soviet Union. We are creating an international image of a gambler who disregards his family's welfare, blinds himself to the future and blanks out the past in a feverish effort to achieve immediate and total security. We are in the midst of a cosmic roll of the dice, with far greater implications than those for an individual gambler.

How do we respond as people of the Kingdom? Do we have anything unique to say to this kind of a world, to this kind of an issue? I hear voices that come out of the Christian community. I have letters, and the general message is, Build more arms and bomb the hell out of them. It is the will of God. It is the battle of Armageddon. It is atheist, godless communism, the devil incarnate against the American Christian nation. Is that the Christian message? I deplore the march of totalitarianism whether it is from the right or from the left. I condemn the brutality of the spiritual bankruptcy of the Soviet system. Are we prepared, however, to abandon everything including the planet itself—all life on the planet—in deference to our anti-communism and myopic anti-Sovietism? That's the decision we as a nation must make today.

How rational individuals can allow themselves to succumb to such bankrupt interpretations of national security, as if our security was vested only in our hardware, is totally beyond my grasp. That's what the Shah of Iran thought, and he had the most sophisticated military machinery and hardware of any country in the Middle East outside of Israel. It didn't save him because he neglected the political, social, and economic problems at home. Our military will not save us as we leave ourselves vulnerable on the economic and political fronts in America today.

There lies our vulnerability; it is not the lack of military hardware. Unfortunately, in my lifetime only one president of the United States understood national security in its totality, in its profound meaning: Dwight Eisenhower. I remember the Democratic candidate for president of the United States in 1960, John F. Kennedy, going across this country picking up votes by the bushel on the scare tactic that somehow the Eisenhower administration had permitted our national defenses to fall to the point that a missile gap existed. No missile gap existed. Our defenses were not down. I remember 1980—twenty years later—a Republican candidate for the presidency going around the country saying the Carter administration had permitted this nation's defenses to fall into dangerous disrepair. If we would elect him, he would secure the nation again. Our defenses are not in disrepair. The numbers games: the Soviet Union has so many launchers, we have so many launchers. They have more; therefore, they must be ahead. It is not the launchers, it's the number of missiles you put on a launch. And we put on more. In addition, it is not the number of missiles on the launch, it's the number of warheads on the missile. And further, it is not the number of warheads on the missile, it's the accuracy of the warheads. In every one of the qualitative analyses, we are ahead. Don't fall for this kind of second-class military armament status that is described to our citizens in order to get more appropriations for military spending.

Where do you think the world would find the help if we had a nuclear holocaust today? Unlike the isolated destruction of Hiroshima, the whole globe would become a Hiroshima and we would become engulfed in a nuclear winter. No nuclear confrontation and triggering of the nuclear attack would come because our administration or the Soviet administration would deliberately press that button. They know the full power of retaliation of either side. What I am concerned about is the fact that in a recent twenty-month period, we had four thousand faulty signals from our advance warning system. One hundred forty-seven of them were serious enough for the alert to be sounded with the submarines at sea, the ICBM silos, and the B-52 pilots. Last year the United States had to remove five thousand people from access to nuclear weapons because of one thing or another: two hundred forty of them for using LSD and heroin on the job; one thousand of them court-martialed for negligence on the job. With all of those people removed from access to nuclear weapons, my concern is an accidental launching. Our advance warning system is more sophisticated even than the Soviet Union's. What kind of faulty signals are they getting from malfunctioning computer chips? That's the kind of world we live in today. That which masquerades as realism is increasingly proving itself removed from reality as we madly pursue the escalation of the nuclear arms race.

Do you know what MX stands for? "Missile experiment," a mere theory. When we move from our present deterrent power base to the first-strike base of the counterforce weapon of the SS18 and SS19 of the Soviet Union and the MX missile of the United States, we have not only moved upward in numbers, but we have also moved to a whole generation of missiles. Instead of aiming our missiles against population centers (that we know they would never tolerate losing) and their aiming missiles against population centers in this country (that we know we would never tolerate losing), we shift those missiles and aim missile to missile. We move to a hair-trigger situation of a pre-emptive strike to destroy their missiles before they can destroy ours. Instead of half an hour to verify those faulty signals from our advance warning systems, we will have six minutes.

What are our alternatives if the future course goes according to plan? The strategic age we are choosing will be characterized by a world bristling with time-urgent, offensive weapons essentially devoid of human control. We will truly have become the servant of the monster. We continue to invest precious resources and billions of dollars into our best minds in an attempt to transform the greatest nightmare imaginable into reality. Four hundred thousand scientists in the U.S. today, and about one-half of the world's scientists, are employed in the development and deployment of nuclear weapons. If one is in an elevator going up and decides to go down, one must stop the elevator first. To get control of this mad rush to global suicide, we have to freeze ourselves where we are in terms of testing, production, and deployment of these new weapons. Once they are out of the laboratories and the production mills it will be too late. Now is the time to freeze the status quo. The first step for mutual reductions is a bilateral, mutually agreed upon status quo freeze; total limitation is necessary.

I urge you to ponder humanity's future with a spiritual dimension equal to that which you direct toward your family, your church and your community. We are of the Kingdom. In the church we are alternately faced with voices appealing to us from very polarized and equally misguided perspectives. Remember, Pontius Pilate was a politician on the move. He knew that if he did a good job in Jerusalem he would be noticed by Caesar. He was starting in the outpost; he knew it was not a place to end up. He probably wanted to end up in the Roman Senate. Who wouldn't? Before he could go anywhere, however, he had to prove his mettle in that very troubled spot in the empire. Confronted with this sticky issue, he tried every tactic of a politician. And, my friend, many of the church people today are studying alternatives and options. First of all, he tried to shift the responsibility to the Jews. Remember when he said you take this man? It didn't work. Then he tried to find a way of escape from the entanglement by releasing Barabbas. That didn't work. Then he tried compromise and had Jesus scourged. Then he tried appeal—crucify your king? That didn't work. Voices in the same way today direct us to trust in the power and political machinations of Caesar with abandon.

Other voices tell us to organize a Christian political action group to attain the levers of Caesar: elect only

Christians to public office and the machine will run. Remember that wonderful saying from John Wesley when he said, "If I'm drowning I'd rather be seen by a burglar who could swim than by a bishop who couldn't"? That's my answer to those who want to form such a group to capture the government. There are those who tell us to "wash your hands of the political battleground and don't get involved. Stay out. You know—that's not the role of the Christian to get involved." As did Pontius Pilate, they are abandoning our Lord's teachings to the mob.

In this world we cannot avoid being political. Christ's politic was demonstrated very clearly through His ministry of love. The Sadducees came to Him and He condemned them because they were blind to the injustices of the time. And then the Zealots came to Him. They wanted to right the injustices with violence; He condemned them equally. For those who want to love Christ and Christianity, dreaming of heaven is to forget that the earth is of God also.

We cannot develop biblical values and a global consciousness without recognizing that the Body of Christ, as the Church universal, is composed of many parts. It's not all an eye. It's not all an ear. Great diversity exists within the Body of Christ. We are part of that beauty and that mystery of diversity because we are a part of the continuing incarnation as God was in Christ reconciling the world. As we are born into the Kingdom by the indwelling of the Holy Spirit, as we receive Christ into our lives, and as we make Christ the Lord of our lives, we become a part of that continuity of Incarnation. That is a mystery and the beauty of the Incarnation. In you, Christ is the glory and the hope of the world. Even in our detachment it is an inadvertent political act to choose that role; we are essentially stepping aside to let others govern in our absence.

Our task, then, is to bring the political realm of our

personal lives under the authority of Jesus Christ. A relationship with God begins with repentance. His will is discovered in our individual lives not through nationalistic vainglory, but in acts of humble love and service and righting the injustices.

Christ, the Servant/Leader, demonstrated the power of leadership by washing the feet of His followers as an act of service. In so doing He demonstrated the truisms and the great verities of the Old Testament as well as asserting the New Covenant of His death, atonement, and resurrection. The prophet Isaiah said, "Is not this the fast that I choose: to loose the bonds of wickedness, to undo the thongs of the yoke, to let the oppressed go free, and to break every yoke? Is it not to share your bread with the hungry, and bring the homeless poor into your house; when you see the naked, to cover him, and not hide yourself from your own flesh?" (Isa. 58:6,7).

Christ demonstrated that truth by His act of Servant/ Leadership. The issues of poverty and weaponry are inexorably coupled; we cannot decouple them. I ask you only to seek the truth. I ask you to not only prayerfully expose your thinking as it may differ from my view, but also to seek from the Scripture and from Christ's ministry and His model what God would have you think and do. I ask you to try therefore to make a difference in an ocean of despair, even though it sometimes may be a sorrowing and disillusioning experience. Unless we have the indwelling of the Holy Spirit to move us ahead, to maintain and sustain us, we will fall by the wayside in discouragement. Only through the power of Jesus Christ can the Kingdom people persevere against all odds. We are not persevering for success, but rather only to demonstrate our faithfulness. We are not given a blueprint for success, but rather instructions to guide us as we lead our lives in an attempt to be the servant/leader. Reinhold Niebuhr said: "Nothing

that is worth doing can be achieved in our lifetime. Therefore we must be saved by hope. Nothing which is true or
beautiful or good makes complete sense in any immediate
context. Therefore we must be saved by faith. So grow
not weary in a pursuit of peace, reconciliation, removing
the injustice wherever it may be found."

No better way exists to encourage you than to use the
words I use for myself when I grow disillusioned and
weary and tired and frustrated. I spent a day with Mother
Teresa in Calcutta a few years ago and came away with a
very warm, loving friendship. When she won the Nobel
Peace Prize, I wrote her a note of congratulations. On her
lined tablet stationery she responded: "Pray for me that I
not loosen my grip on the hand of Jesus even under the
guise of ministering to the poor."

Even under the guise of working for peace we cannot
lose our grip. I remember on that day saying to her, "Don't
you grow discouraged when you look around and see this
utter, abject poverty, the hellhole of all the globe, Calcutta, and how little you are able to really accomplish in
relieving the misery of human starvation and disease?"
She smiled and she said, "Oh, no. For you see the Lord
has not called me to be successful. He has called me to be
faithful." This is our call.

Chapter Ten

Can War Bring Peace?
A Reexamination of the Just-War Theory in the Nuclear Age
by Richard J. Mouw

Recently I read yet another account of John Calvin's debates with the Anabaptists in the sixteenth century. I was once again taken aback by the anger and resentment and the extensive bearing of false witness which characterized those discussions on both sides of the dispute. The same kind of acrimony later characterized the debates between the Puritans and the Quakers.

As evangelical Christians, many of us are the physical and/or spiritual descendants of those past antagonists. And when we add to this consideration the fact that many of us are also the descendants of slaves and slave owners, of oppressors and the oppressed, of Christians who have fought in opposing armies in many wars, then we really cannot avoid acknowledging that our evangelical dialogue on the issues of war and peace is a very important and long overdue ecumenical event. We are dealing here with the issues which have been far more divisive in the Christian community than our past and continuing discussions of infant versus adult baptism or free will versus predestination.

And yet evangelical Christians still seem strangely reluctant to discuss these matters in a humble and mutually-accepting manner. We seem content to eye each other's positions warily and from a distance, refusing to acknowledge the need to struggle together before the Word of God, seeking to know the will of the Lord of life for this crucial area of human activity.

This should not be. Our allegiance is not to any political ideology, governmental program or military policy, but to Jesus Christ who saved us and incorporated us into the fellowship of believers. To belong to Jesus Christ and to His Body on earth requires a willingness to be open to dialogue and mutual correction. It is especially important that in these days, in which the nations of the earth have built up arsenals capable of causing unspeakable destruction, that God's people—whatever their present views about the proper use of military violence—struggle together to understand more clearly the will of God for these times.

With this need in mind, I will offer some observations here about the perspective on the issues of war and peace which is associated with the Just-War theory. I will try to explain why it is that I think this theory to be a helpful instrument for Christians to employ in understanding their mission of peacemaking. But I will also offer some words of caution about how this theory ought to be used by Christians. It is not likely that Christians—even Christians who profess a common allegiance to the authority of God's Word—will settle all of their differences about these matters in the near future. But it does seem important to look for a common ground on which we can stand together as we witness to the power of the gospel of peace. My comments here are meant as a contribution to that search.

REASONS FOR ACCEPTING THE JUST-WAR THEORY

Many of us are not pacifists. We believe that governments have been invested by God with the authority to use the sword both in the internal policing of the affairs of nations and in the defense of nations against external enemies. We also believe that there are circumstances in which citizens are justified in taking up the sword against their own governments, when those governments have become agents of systematic oppression.

In allowing for these kinds of activities, we do not mean to be suggesting that there is a permissible kind of violence which can take place "outside of the perfection of Christ." We mean to say that there are occasions in which Christians are permitted, perhaps even obligated, to take up the sword in pursuit of just and righteous goals.

But we also want to insist that there are limits to the use of violence on the part of both governments and revolutionary groups. Just-War theorists have insisted that moral considerations must be brought to bear on the use of military violence. One set of considerations has to do with the process of entering into military activity. Any government or group which is considering military engagement must ask questions of this sort: Is the cause being fought for a legitimate one? Is the intention in undertaking military action morally proper? Have all the other means of pursuing the stated goals been exhausted? Is there a reasonable hope of achieving goals by military means? Is the military action approved by legitimate authorities in accordance with proper procedures?

A second set of questions has to do with the actual pursuit of military policies. Here Just-War theorists have insisted on questions of this sort: Are the military means being used proportionate to the goals being pursued? Are the means themselves morally proper? And is the violence employed a discriminatory violence? That is, is it targeted primarily against combatants rather than noncombatants?

These questions are a means of fleshing out a basic principle which underlies the Just-War theory. The principle is this: that the use of lethal violence is under certain conditions morally justified.

This is, of course, the basic principle which is disputed by pacifists. But to many of us it seems to be a proper principle to accept for several reasons. Each of these reasons requires a much lengthier defense than I can give here. But I will attempt to explain briefly the kinds of grounds which defenders of the Just-War theory appeal to in defending their position.

First, *this principle seems to be one which can be defended on the basis of the Scriptures.* In debates with pacifists, defenders of Just-War doctrine are fond of pointing to God's sanction of violence in the Old Testament. This line of argument seems convincing to me. However we interpret God's *intentions* in permitting—and sometimes even commanding—Israel to engage in violent military campaigns, it seems to many of us that it is a clear fact of Old Testament history that God did endorse the use of violence.

Many pacifists counter this appeal to the Old Testament by pointing to the New Testament, and especially the teachings of Jesus. Doesn't the Sermon on the Mount manifest a very different spirit than that which we find in the Old Testament? Isn't the call to Christian discipleship a challenge to lay down the sword and take up the cross?

When the argument focuses exclusively on the teachings of Jesus, we Just-War defenders experience—if we are honest—our most awkward moments in debating these matters. Nonetheless, for many of us this sense of awkwardness does not succeed in shaking us from our basic conviction that the use of lethal violence is on occasion morally justified. We want an understanding of the Sermon on the Mount which fits into what we take to be the overall sense of the Scriptures. This involves not only looking at Jesus' teachings in the light of the Old Testament background but also in relation to the apostolic witness and the life of the early Church.

Second, *this principle*—that lethal violence is on occasion morally justified—*seems to square with the demands of our moral experience.* Consider an example. A terrorist is holding a large group of school children hostage. He refuses to release them unless certain demands are met— demands which are morally repugnant and practically impossible. He has begun to execute two of these children each hour: six of them are already dead, and many more will die if the terrorist is not stopped. I have a high-powered rifle with telescopic lens at my disposal, and suddenly I see the terrorist standing with his back to the window. Should I pull the trigger? Would doing so be a violation of the demands of discipleship?

As a Christian who has attempted to allow the gospel to shape my moral sensitivities, I must report that I would pull the trigger in such a situation. I see nothing in the Scriptures which would prohibit me from doing so. And I am not alone in this conviction. Many Christian persons possessing what I consider to be "sanctified consciences" concur in this judgment. This seems to me to be a weighty consideration.

Third, *subscribing to the underlying principle of the Just-War theory seems to provide Christians with a basis for offering helpful, practical advice with regard to military policies.* In many historical situations, the practical issue faced by governments is not *whether* or not to employ violence.

Rather, it is *how much* violence is to be employed. A commitment to the principle underlying the Just-War theory allows Christians to enter into this latter kind of debate. It permits Christians to acknowledge that governments do in fact have a legitimate right to use the sword in pursuing the work of justice and peace. On the basis of this acknowledgment, Christians may then argue for policies in which the sword is being *properly* used.

Again, none of these arguments will be convincing, as stated, to Christian pacifists. They can respond by arguing that we Just-War theorists have not properly grasped the overall sense of the Scriptures, nor are our consciences properly sanctified, nor are we giving good advice to governments. These are challenges which must be taken seriously by Just-War theorists. But I am convinced that a plausible case can be made for the three considerations which I have briefly outlined.

CAUTIONARY GUIDELINES

It is necessary to insist, however, that the Just-War theory be used with great caution. It has not always been used cautiously in the past. Indeed it has been put to many bad, even wicked, uses. If the errors of the past are to be avoided, a number of cautionary notes must be sounded.

First, *it is important to emphasize that the Just-War theory must be understood as an instrument of peacemaking.* Indeed, this is an area of Christian discussion in which the terminology that is used is very unfortunate. Some Christian groups are referred to as "peace churches." Others, who disagree with pacifism, are labelled "Just-War defenders." Thus the impression is given that some of us have a vested interest in defending and promoting wars.

All Christians are called to be followers of the Prince of Peace. A concern for peacemaking ought not to be the exclusive property of pacifists. A Christian can never be a defender of war as such. The real debate, properly understood, must be about the proper strategies of peacemaking.

Historically, the Just-War theory had its origins in a desire to promote peace. Christian thinkers first attempted to formulate a Just-War theory against the background of a history of unbridled, no-holds-barred militarism. These thinkers intended to impose some sort of checks on the use of military violence.

One very crucial concern among Christian Just-War theorists has been a desire for peace. War, in their view, was only permissible if it was a means of attaining some measure of peace among nations. The Just-War theory was intended as an instrument for reducing the number of wars and for placing limits on the violence which occurred within those wars. This is clearly the spirit of John Calvin's remarks on the use of military violence:

> But it is the duty of all magistrates here to guard particularly against giving vent to their passions even in the slightest degree. Rather, if they have to punish, let them not be carried away with headlong anger, or be seized with hatred, or burn with implacable severity. Let them also (as Augustine says) have pity on the common nature in the one whose special fault they are punishing. Or, if they must arm themselves against the enemy, that is, the armed robber, let them not lightly seek occasion to do so; indeed, let them not accept the occasion when offered, unless they are driven to it by extreme necessity. For if we must perform much more than the heathen philosopher required when he wanted war to seem a seeking of peace, surely everything else ought to be tried before recourse is had to arms. Lastly, in both situations

let them not allow themselves to be swayed by any private affection, but be led by concern for the people alone. Otherwise, they very wickedly abuse their power, which has been given them not for their own advantage, but for the benefit and service of others (*Institutes, IV, XX,* 12).

It is especially important in this regard for Just-War theorists to avoid the sinful spirit of militarism. Militarism is the glorification of the military, a basic trust in military might and military means. In its worst form, militarism is a worship of the military, an ultimate devotion to the gods of war. But there are other less "absolute" versions of militarism. Militarism can involve a fondness for military solutions to urgent problems, or a spirit of vengeance which can only be satisfied by military victories.

The Bible consistently condemns militarism in its various forms. We must not place any kind of ultimate or strong trust in military might. "Woe to those who go down to Egypt for help and rely on horses, who trust in chariots because they are many and in horsemen because they are very strong, and do not look to the Holy One of Israel or consult the Lord!" (Isa. 31:1).

The Bible repeatedly warns us against idolatry—the placing of our trust in some dimension of the creaturely. The military has been, throughout human history, a strong candidate for idolatrous trust. The military can easily become characterized by pride in its own strength, and it calls upon others to put their trust in that strength. And, historically, the military has shown a talent for calling upon other social institutions—religion, education, business, government—to reinforce its claims.

The phenomenon of militarism ought to be a matter of continuing concern to the Christian community. The biblical record itself offers countless examples of the sin of militaristic arrogance and pride—the distortion and misuse of whatever power it is which rightly belongs to the military. It was, after all, the military which carried out the crucifixion of the Son of God. And the final encounter of the ages will be one in which the kings of the earth gather their armies and assemble their most destructive weapons, in league with corrupt merchants in the service of the blasphemous Beast, to conduct the ultimate assault on the Lamb of God.

But a recognition of the idolatry of militarism is not sufficient grounds for opposing all that the military says and does. Other institutions—the family, the church, the government, even a college or a seminary—can make false claims for itself; each of these social powers and institutions can become an idol, it can be characterized by arrogance and pride, it can call for ultimate allegiance to its own means and goals. But this does not mean that these institutions have no legitimate place in human life. And it is precisely this issue of the *proper* use of military power which the Just-War theory is meant to address.

Secondly, *Just-War doctrine, properly understood, is an attempt to be faithful to the biblical command that we love our neighbors.* This is an important point to make in discussion with pacifist Christians who often assume that we Just-War theorists are operating with some sort of "double ethic"—an ethic that attempts to synthesize a biblical love of our fellow human beings with extra-biblical moral principles. And, indeed, some defenders of Just Wars have often made their case along such lines. The commands of Christ, they have argued, are noble principles; but we also need moral guidelines which help us to be "realistic."

There is nothing in the Just-War theory which requires us to pursue that kind of formulation. Many of us who subscribe to that tradition want to insist that military violence can on occasion be a *means* of fulfilling the commands of Christ. The 1983 pastoral letter of the Roman Catholic bishops is very helpful in this regard. The bishops argue— and correctly, I believe—that "the command of love" must be "understood as the need to restrain an enemy who would injure the innocent." Love requires that on occasion we take up arms to protect our innocent neighbors against the oppressor.

The requirement that we love our neighbors cannot be separated from other biblical commands. The Bible also tells us that we must act justly; it tells us that we must seek righteousness. The justice and righteousness which we must promote must be grounded in the love of our human neighbors. But it is also correct to say that love must *issue in* acts of justice and righteousness. When we encounter a situation in which one of our neighbors is harming another of our neighbors, we must ask what pattern of justice the love of our neighbors requires in that situation. And it may very well be that we must use violent means to show our love for the oppressed neighbor.

Third, *it must also be admitted that the Just-War doctrine is a dangerous doctrine*. This has been implied in other things which have already been said here; but the point must be made explicit.

One can admit that a doctrine is dangerous without thereby repudiating that doctrine. Doctrines can be true yet dangerous. A theory may be accurate in itself but difficult to apply accurately. Consider a parallel moral example. Suppose that a German Christian male had the opportunity during Hitler's reign to form an adulterous relationship with Eva Braun, Hitler's mistress, and thereby gain important information which might well lead to the downfall of the Third Reich. It is at least conceivable, I believe, that this might constitute a case of Just Adultery. But suppose—and it is very interesting that we have often been much stricter with the adultery commandment than we have with the killing commandment—that having recognized the legitimacy of such a rare undertaking, Christians went on to formulate a Just-Adultery doctrine, specifying those rare conditions under which a Christian might justifiably commit an act of adultery for a noble and righteous cause.

Such a doctrine on my hypothesis might very well be legitimate and proper. But suppose that this doctrine also created a tendency toward unjustified adultery—merely by officially acknowledging the fact that under certain conditions adultery might be morally justified. Suppose further that people were then trained to commit adultery in the event that their services might become necessary. Suppose also that special medals of honor were awarded to outstanding adulterers.

Well, we need not follow through on the implications of such a doctrine. But the point should be clear: some doctrines, however true and appropriate they might be in application to rare cases, become dangerous when they are propagated and institutionalized. They can themselves become a lure to sin. They can themselves become instruments of our rebellion before the face of God. And Just-War defenders would do well to consider the actual historical uses and the psychological tendencies of their Just-War teaching.

Fourth, *Just-War doctrine cannot be isolated from a larger ethical context.* Just-War theory insists that certain questions must be asked about the use of military violence. I listed these questions earlier; some of them apply to the question of whether a government can initiate a military campaign, and others deal with the proper use of violence within such a campaign.

But it would be wrong to think that people should only raise moral questions about matters of war and peace when they are either about to embark upon a war or are already in the midst of a war. There must be ethical preparation for applying those concerns to military situations.

Consider a parallel in marriage relations. Husbands and wives often argue with each other. Marital fighting can often be an element of a very healthy marriage relationship. But there are fair and unfair ways of fighting with one's spouse. It is even possible to spell out some rules for fair marital fighting. Even if we had such rules to go by, however, they would not necessarily be very helpful in the actual process of marital fighting. Arguments between spouses can get very heated; when we are in the midst of such an argument we are not always in the best mood to think about the rules of fair play.

The best time to utilize rules of fairness for marital arguments is when we are not in the midst of an argument. We must think about those rules in our calmer moments, and attempt to "internalize" them, to allow them to shape our attitudes and instincts. Then perhaps they will serve us in those moments when we are not explicitly thinking about them.

Similarly, Just-War criteria must be reflected upon and "internalized" by military planners during times of peace. They must shape the attitudes and dispositions of those whose task it is to make military decisions, so that in the heat of war they will act out of an intelligent desire to act justly toward their enemies.

There is another sense in which the use of Just-War criteria requires ethical preparation. Moral deliberations on the proper use of military violence must function in the context of a longer-range moral commitment to keeping the peace. If a nation conducts its foreign policy in a morally irresponsible manner, so that its relations deteriorate to the point where military action is necessary, it has already violated its moral responsibilities. To begin thinking morally about the proper use of military violence at that point is not especially praiseworthy. An allegiance to Just-War doctrine does not imply that moral considerations must only be introduced at those points where the question of violence has become a pressing one.

If Just-War doctrine is to be a proper ethical tool for Christians, it must be rooted in the life of prayer and in an immersion in the study of the Scriptures. The Christian use of Just-War criteria cannot be introduced in an *ad hoc* manner. These criteria must be accompanied by a fundamental commitment to justice, righteousness, and peace. They must be used in the context of a careful, Spirit-guided study of our historical context, so that we may discern what the Lord is calling us to say and do. Christian decisions about the proper use of violence must be of a piece with the rest of our lives—lives devoted to the service of God and neighbor.

Christians need a larger dynamic ethical context for our reflections on the question of war and peace—a context in which we think about these things in the light of the whole of God's Law for our lives. Just-War criteria cannot operate in an ethical vacuum. For example, the moral questions regarding a possible military confrontation between the United States and the Soviet Union are not exhausted by the questions associated with Just-War doctrine. Americans must also ask whether we have borne false witness against our Soviet neighbors. Have we been fair in attributing certain motives to them? Have we represented their actions properly? Have we coveted their influence in the world? Have our policies toward them been rooted in our own nationalistic pride? Do they have legitimate complaints against us with regard to our own behavior in the community of nations? We cannot separate Just-War questions from the full range of ethical deliberation.

Fifth, *Just-War thinking must be linked to a larger theological context.* It must be rooted in an acceptance of the full range of biblical teaching if it is to function properly for Christians. Evangelical Christians have talked much about the need for "sound theology." But we have done little by way of developing a carefully formulated theological framework for dealing with the issues of war and peace.

PEACEMAKING THEOLOGY

What would such a theology of peacemaking look like? I will note some of the major features here.

First, *it must be a theology which is grounded in a belief in divine creation.* Evangelical Christians have been ardent defenders of "creationism." But we have often limited our attention to the implications of a belief in divine creation for biological theory. Indeed, we have often put forth very questionable claims in this area with a much stronger air of certainty than seems to be permitted on the basis of biblical givens.

However that may be, a concern to live in faithfulness as a biblical witness to the fact of divine creation must go well beyond an attention to the details of biological and geological theory. Biblical creationists must have more than a creationist science. They must also develop a creationist ethic, a creationist technology, a creationist politics, and so on.

One of the great creationist texts in the Scriptures is Psalm 24:1: "The earth is the Lord's and the fulness thereof, the world and those who dwell therein." The world in which we live is God's world. It is not ours to do with what we please. Human beings are called to be stewards of the good creation. God wants us to cultivate the world in order to bring out what is best in it.

And above all we are to respect human life as the crowning achievement of God's creation. This is why many of us are so strongly opposed to abortion-on-demand. But our respect for the created dignity of human life must also extend to a concern about the destructive potential of present-day military technology. Just-War theory embodies this respect in its insistence that military means must be proportionate to the ends being sought, and in its prohibition of indiscriminate military violence. But a Christian theology of creation must pour very specific content into these concerns.

Second, *our theology of peacemaking must be one in which the fall into sin is taken seriously.* We have already noted the ways in which a recognition of the legitimate role of the military can degenerate into a spirit of militarism. The Bible makes it very clear that fallen human beings are prone to evil. Both individuals and groups are easily lured into patterns of pride and self-deception. Our military activities are not immune to these sinful tendencies. This is an area where Christians must be constantly on guard against the onslaughts of the Evil One. Defenders of the Just-War theory—since they do not automatically rule out all military activity as sinful—must be especially vigilant in this regard.

North American Evangelicals have been very selective in their application of the doctrine of original sin to international relations. We have been very rigorous in our insistence that the Soviet leadership is sinful: "You can't trust the Russians!" Therefore, we have argued, it is necessary for the United States to maintain its huge stockpile of nuclear weapons.

If, however, we are to be evenhanded—as the Scriptures surely are—in applying the doctrine of original sin to the arms race, the argument must also cut in the other direction. Given the fact that we Americans are sinners, can we trust ourselves with this vast destructive weaponry? Are our own leaders immune not only to the limits and errors of human finitude but also to the sinful tendencies toward self-deception and rebellion? These questions become especially poignant when we consider the fact that there is only one nation in the history of humankind which has actually used an atomic or nuclear weapon in an aggressive attack on another nation—and that nation was not the Soviet Union.

Third, *our theology of peacemaking must also focus on the redemption which has been accomplished in Jesus Christ.* There are many aspects of the cross and resurrection of Christ which have a bearing on this subject. Of special importance here are the implications of Jesus' redemptive ministry for our understanding of our relationships to the nations of the world.

The blood of Jesus makes us into a new kind of people. This is clearly proclaimed in the song which the saints sing to the Lamb in Revelation 5:9,10: "Worthy art thou to take the scroll and to open its seals, for thou wast slain and by thy blood didst ransom men for God from every tribe and tongue and people and nation, and hast made them a kingdom and priests to our God, and they shall reign on earth."

God saves each of us individually, but in saving us He incorporates us into a new kind of multi-ethnic, multi-cultural, multinational community. Because of the blood of Christ we may never again boast of other "bloods"—we may never again take pride in having "white blood," or in being a "red-blooded male," or in having been "defended by the American blood shed on the battlefields of the world." Our hope rests solely on the blood of Christ.

Our new identity as disciples of the Lamb, then, "relativizes" all of our other commitments and allegiances. It makes us members of that "holy nation" which is the Church, whose citizens are presently scattered among the existing nations of the earth. This citizenship carries with it obligations which override those duties which we have to the temporal nations in which we live. We belong to all who confess the name of Christ: Soviet peasants, Polish laborers, black African mineworkers, Vietnamese farmers.

In a word, the gospel ought to provide us with "internationalist" sensitivities. And these sensitivities will regularly raise profound questions about our involvement in military conflicts. In many cases it will not be easy to solve these conflicts. But the obligations to struggle with them is very real.

Finally, *our theology of peacemaking must give expression to our hope for the future reign of Christ.* We know that Christ will someday return as victorious King, and that every knee will bow before Him. The tyrants and unjust governments of the present age will not be ultimately victorious. Christians do not need to fear, in any basic way, "the Soviet threat" because they know that nothing that the Soviets or any other group can do will thwart God's plan.

As we utilize the Just-War theory, then, we ought not to allow fear or vengeance to control our thinking. We do not have to accept the burden of making everything turn out right in human history. We are not called to *be* gods, but to *serve* the one true God.

This does not mean that we can stand by passively as history unfolds. We are called to be active agents of justice and peace. But it does mean that we will pursue our active ministries of righteousness with very different motives and purposes than those whose thinking is controlled by the "minds" of the present age. And foundational to our attitudes regarding war and peace will be the confidence that God intends to cover the whole creation with His peace, His *shalom.* All of our actions and programs and strategies must be faithful expressions of that hope.

CONCLUSION

I have tried to explain why I subscribe to the Just-War theory. I have also tried to show that a Christian who holds to this theory will do so in a very cautious manner. Indeed, if Christian defenders of the Just-War perspective were to use the theory in the way in which I have described it, they would find that the gap between themselves and Christian pacifists has been significantly narrowed.

This is as it should be. And it is especially important to see how this gap has narrowed in the nuclear age. Just-War theorists cannot simply reject nuclear weapons out of hand. They are committed to a careful examination of the technological details so that they can weigh those factors in the light of Just-War criteria. In doing so, they must consider three very important questions: Is it ever permissible for a nation to initiate a nuclear attack against another nation? Is it even permissible for a nation to respond to such an attack with destructive nuclear force? And, is it permissible for a nation to maintain large stockpiles of nuclear weapons, even if it never intends to use them?

I am convinced that Just-War considerations require a negative answer to the first two questions. With regard to the third question we may have to grant some legitimacy (as did the Roman Catholic bishops) to the idea of a "nuclear deterrence." But even here we must acknowledge that it is necessary for Christians to work diligently toward bringing the arms race to a halt.

The risks of peacemaking in our present nuclear context are great. But the risks associated with our present course of nuclear buildup are even greater. The time has come for all Christians, whatever their views on the legitimate use of military violence, to find common and concrete ways of working together for the cause of peace.

Chapter Eleven

The Challenge of Nehemiah
We Need to Rebuild the Walls of America's Defensive System
by William Armstrong

On Monday, May 23, 1983, the police arrested 242 singing, flower-waving Christians as they knelt to pray in the rotunda of the United States Capitol. They had come to protest the MX missile and had deliberately chosen to visit the rotunda for that purpose because it is an area where such demonstrations are forbidden. They wanted to dramatize their concerns for U.S. nuclear policy.

About forty-eight hours later, the United States Senate, including a number of Bible-believing Christians, voted by an overwhelming margin to approve the MX missile. These two events, in the same place, just two days apart, dramatize and symbolize the deep and keenly felt differences of opinion among believers and other Americans about the right course of action for Americans in the nuclear age.

Some Christians affirm pacifism. Others emphasize deterrence. Many support, perhaps with reservations, the Just War. For my own part, I admire and respect those who conscientiously advocate pacifism, although I do not share their view. I support with some reservations the notion of deterrence. I support the Just War but I do so with great reservations.

However, I must say that in all of these thoughts, though they are worthy, I do not find any that give my own heart a very great sense of hope and optimism. On the contrary, I find in myself and I sense among others, a growing sense of frustration—a growing sense that somehow we are hurtling at high speed to the end of some kind of intellectual cul-de-sac. I believe there are people who have been praying as I have, "Lord, haven't you got some better options than anything we have considered so far?"

I have to believe there are better options. But I am afraid that many of us have been so preoccupied with the status quo—either to overthrow the status quo or to somehow sustain the status quo—that we have not been able to look seriously at other options which exist.

For the past two decades, our country has been committed to a policy known as Mutual Assured Destruction (MAD), a doctrine which I earnestly believe to be impractical and unrealistic, which does not achieve the goal of nuclear deterrence, which is anathema to pacifism, and which violates the basic principles of the Just War doctrine. If there were ever a policy which in intellectually and morally bankrupt, it is the official policy of our country— Mutual Assured Destruction.

The essence of the MAD doctrine is quite simple. As a matter of national policy we choose not to defend our homeland. We once had squadrons of interceptor aircraft to defend against manned bomber attack. We have grounded those interceptor squadrons. We once had an antiballistic missile system to protect, at least in some measure, against incoming intercontinental-ballistic missiles (ICBMs). We have disbanded that antiballistic missile force.

It is our policy *not* to defend our homeland. Not to defend our civilian population against nuclear attack. Instead, we leave ourselves deliberately unprotected and then we threaten the assured destruction of the Soviet Union if they attack us. Now, what we are saying is that we are prepared to hold in hostage the lives of tens and scores of millions of people in this country and the Soviet Union in some kind of theoretical balance of terror.

According to my study of history, no other nation in all of recorded time has ever adopted such a policy. I have been reading a lot of military history over the last year or so, and I cannot find one single instance where a major nation has, as a deliberate, conscious decision of national policy said, "We are not going to defend our homeland."

I believe military historians would agree there is not one case where a major nation has said, "We are not going to defend our people or our homeland." And for very good reason. The policy of Mutual Assured Destruction is unrealistic.

The first false premise on which the MAD doctrine was based was the notion that the intercontinental ballistic missile of the late 1960s vintage was the ultimate weapon. The MADmen assumed there would be no further advances in military technology, at least none that would matter.

It was an assumption that proved false within a few years after Secretary of State Robert McNamara succeeded in making Mutual Assured Destruction official U.S. policy. The development of independently targetable warheads with circular errors probable of three hundred feet or less undermined an essential component of the MAD doctrine. With accurate multiple independently-targeted reentry vehicles (MIRVs) on ICBMs, it was at least theoretically possible for one nation to destroy the other's weapons under condition of surprise attack. Assured destruction no longer would be mutual.

Another fundamental flaw of mutual assured destruction is that it was never mutual. Soviet leaders, in both official statements for foreign consumption and in their military journals, derided it from the beginning as both insane and immoral. For the MAD doctrine to have any validity at all, it is necessary for the leaders of both the United States and the Soviet Union to reject nuclear war as an instrument of policy. We, of course, have done so. But the Soviet leaders never have. On the contrary, it is still Soviet doctrine that a military clash between the Communist world and the capitalist world is inevitable; that weapons of mass destruction will be used in that clash, and that the Soviets should initiate the use of weapons of mass destruction in order to make certain that the Socialist world will emerge triumphant. It is their policy to protect themselves and assure a survival of their country, their industrial base, and a large proportion of their civilian population.

They have got a long way to go in reaching that goal. But they have made very significant progress. And the closer they get to being able to perfect a defense of their homeland, the more unstable the world situation becomes if we remain unprotected, if we do not undertake to at least defend ourselves. If they should ever reach the point where they feel they have near capacity to prevent us from retaliation under the Mutual Assured Destruction doctrine, they might be tempted to run the risk of war.

The practical reasons I have discussed are more than reason enough for us to abandon, once and for all, the doctrine of MAD. But there is for me an even more compelling reason: the MAD doctrine is immoral. There is something macabre, and worse, in basing our security on our ability to murder Russian women and children. And it is even more reprehensible—if that is possible—to deliberately increase the exposure of our own people to nuclear destruction simply in order to fulfill the demands of an abstract, ahistorical, unproven, and illogical theory. We pray that deterrence will not fail. But if deterrence fails, there is nothing to be gained by massacring ordinary Russian civilians, the vast majority of whom have suffered more from communism, and who hate communism more than we ever will.

There has been much talk in the press and elsewhere that there is no such thing as a defense against a nuclear attack. In my opinion, that is simply not true. On March 23, 1983, President Ronald Reagan suggested a 180-degree shift in our policy of Mutual Assured Destruction and urged Americans to think for the first time in a couple of decades about defending our homeland. He advocated a policy which, if adopted, would greatly enhance not only U.S. security but the stability of the international situation.

If we can create an effective ballistic missile defense, the American people no longer need fear a nuclear holocaust. We can lift that fear from the lives of all of our people without relying for our security on the goodwill and humanitarianism of leaders who have butchered innocents from Afghanistan to Poland, or on the promises of totalitarian leaders who have never kept such promises in the past.

There are several different kinds of homeland defense. One of the most promising of the systems now under consideration is the so-called High Frontier concept. In essence it is a purely defensive concept. It is non-nuclear; it has no offensive capability whatsoever; it could not threaten any nation, large or small; it is designed only to intercept and destroy incoming ballistic missiles.

Some criticize and say, "Well, High Frontier or other ballistic missile defense will never work." Maybe they are right, but I do not think so. An effective missile defense system need not be perfect in order to achieve a substantial reduction in danger. The evidence is increasingly clear that this is a practical option.

But it is not the practical issue I want to address so much as the moral question which lies behind and above the practical. Every possible Christian moral value that bears on this subject seems to me violated by reliance on our current strategy of Mutual Assured Destruction. The means are not just and proportional; they do not hold out the promise of a better peace; they do not discriminate between combatant and non-combatant. In every way, it seems to me, we have got to search for something better.

Furthermore, if we can create an effective ballistic missile defense, we can then begin to withdraw from our own arsenal the weapons of mass destruction that have cast such a pall over the world. If we can base our security on something more substantial than our ability to kill Russian women and children, we need no longer stockpile such weapons. We could take a very positive step toward reducing the number of offensive weapons in the world without fear of endangering our own security, and perhaps begin the process that would remove these nightmare weapons from the face of the earth.

Twenty-five hundred years ago, one of the most charismatic and courageous figures of antiquity came out of Susa to Jerusalem. He had a burning desire to rebuild the walls of Jerusalem. He was a great leader of men. And yet he saw himself as utterly dependent upon the God of heaven. Of course, I'm referring to Nehemiah. I think we ought to at least consider him as a role model of a peacemaker because Nehemiah created a defensive system. He rebuilt the walls to defend—no offensive capability there—just to defend.

We ought to critically examine Nehemiah's actions and motives. He did not threaten massive retaliation. He did not say mutual assured destruction. Interestingly enough, neither did Nehemiah negotiate with Sanballat for a reduction in weapons and spears and chariots and so on. He built the walls. He would not permit the civilian population to be held hostage to the good intentions and peaceability of Jerusalem's enemies.

And let us note well that Nehemiah prayed. He prayed and prayed and prayed and prayed. He confessed the sins of his country and his people.` And his own sins.

When President Reagan identified the Soviet Union as an evil regime in his controversial remarks to the National Association of Evangelicals in Orlando, Florida, he was correct. The Soviet Union has killed sixty million people. They have millions of political and religious prisoners in gulags. They are threatening war and exporting revolution around the world. They are ruthlessly repressing the people of Poland and Eastern Europe. They are guilty of atrocities in Cambodia and Afghanistan and elsewhere, and I do not believe that God gave us brains and the capacity for moral judgment to remain indifferent or silent about that kind of evil in the world.

But at the same time, Barbara Williams Skinner had it right when in her speech at the Pasadena conference she said, "This does not give us the license to hate the Russian people or to depersonalize them or to begin to think of them, even inadvertently, as the targets for nuclear weapons. They are potentially our brothers and sisters. They are souls to be won for Christ."

Neither can we fail to identify the regime as evil in the world. If we do so, if we remain silent about that, in my judgment we are guilty of the same kind of moral myopia that permitted Hitler to slaughter millions while the so-called civilized nations remained silent.

However, having noted the evil of other nations, we must also confess our own sins. We must admit that we are deeply flawed not only in our individual lives but as a nation. This richly blessed nation has turned to false gods. We have erected idols. We permit abortion, euthanasia, infanticide, materialism, decadent moral standards, pornography, racism, cults, mysticism, complacency. We have much to confess.

Nehemiah prayed, confessed, he informed himself, he reformed the civil practices of Jerusalem. He restored the Sabbath and the tithes and the sacred practices. One of my prayers is that we, as evangelical Christians, will develop the same kind of courage and determination that Nehemiah had—to inform ourselves; to join in a great crusade to reform the political practices; to restore the spiritual life of America and to become the vanguard of renewal in our country and the world. May we pray as we have never prayed before, and then, having done so, think about High Frontier and homeland defense and Mutual Assured Destruction and pacifism and the Just War and make the best decision we can, recognizing full well that the Prince of Peace did not say any of these things.

He did not say Mutual Assured Destruction or High Frontier or pacifism. He said, "All authority in heaven and on earth has been given to me. Go therefore and make disciples of all nations, baptizing them in the name of the Father and of the Son and of the Holy Spirit" (Matt. 28:18,19).

For peacemakers the ultimate issue is simply this. We can change the world only as we can change men's lives and only Jesus Christ can change men's lives.

Chapter Twelve

Keeping the Peace with Nuclear Deterrence

by   Edmund W. Robb

Matthew 5:9: "Blessed are the peacemakers, for they shall be called the sons of God."

John 14:27: "Peace I leave with you; my peace I give to you; not as the world gives do I give to you. Let not your hearts be troubled, neither let them be afraid."

May we never forget that as evangelical Christians we have a dual citizenship—our citizenship and ultimate loyalty is in heaven, but we are also citizens of this world with its responsibilities and obligations. Good Christians recognize their stewardship for time and eternity.

There is no issue of greater importance than the question of peace. Of course, we all want peace. The only question for Christians is, How do we achieve it?

Can we address questions of high urgency and inevitable controversy in a way that strengthens rather than weakens our fellowship? It is important that Evangelicals have unity in diversity. Let us recognize the integrity of those who disagree with us. Creative tension can be healthy. Hopefully it will force us to do our homework and think clearly. Perhaps we shall learn from one another. Let us be open and willing to consider the positions of other committed Christians.

Timothy Smith has said, "The biblical way of seeking truth is not through polarized dialectics but through moral and spiritual community." We should stipulate that everyone in the dialogue does care; we are not in a commitment competition nor counting who sheds more tears for an imperiled planet.

Let us approach the problem of peacemaking with humility. History amply demonstrates that church bodies have no special ability to analyze political problems. Certainly we have transcendent principles. Hopefully we have been sensitized by the Holy Spirit. Therefore, the temptation is to speak with a moral arrogance and unattractive self-righteousness! Let us listen to others and consider the possibility that we may be wrong.

A prevailing theme of Scripture is *peace*. Indeed, a fruit of the Spirit is peace. Jesus gives peacemaking a high priority: Matthew 5:9 shows this. But James reminds us of the source of strife: "What causes wars, and what causes fightings among you? Is it not your passions that are at war in your members? You desire and do not have; so you kill. And you covet and cannot obtain; so you fight and wage war" (Jas. 4:1,2). As Evangelicals may we never forget that the root problem is sin! We have the answer in Christ Jesus. Let us proclaim His salvation to the ends of the earth.

However, this does not excuse us from giving attention to the manifestation of humanity's rebellion against God. Every enlightened Christian must work to alleviate injustice, oppression, inequities, and poverty which sow seeds of war.

Let us recognize the waste of military expenditures and manpower. According to Dr. Robert Jastrow, the internationally-known scientist and authority on life in the cosmos and past director of NASA's Goddard Institute for Space Studies:

> SALT Treaty or no, the Soviet Union continued to outspend the United States by a wide margin on bombs and missiles throughout the 1970s. The United States' budget for strategic forces— bombs, missiles, bombers, and submarines— went down under the Nixon, Ford and Carter administrations, and reached a low point of about nine billion dollars in 1979, at which time it was three-tenths of one percent of our Gross National Product. Meanwhile, Russian spending on missiles and bombs continued at a level of about forty billion dollars a year. By that time, the Soviet Union had spent about one trillion dollars on nuclear weapons.[1]

This is sheer madness. Think what could be done to improve the human condition if 90 percent of the military budget of the NATO powers and the Soviet Union were given to building roads, schools, hospitals and public services. If 10 percent of this money were available to send missionaries, teachers, and doctors rather than soldiers, the task of world evangelization could be completed.

As Christians we must work not only for nuclear disarmament, but for total, biological, chemical disarmament of all weapons of mass destruction.

As Evangelicals, however, let us remember that there

will be no permanent peace apart from the Prince of Peace. As long as there is rebellion in the hearts of humanity there will be strife among peoples. Our task, along with spiritual salvation, is to keep the potential destruction limited and to find alternate political ways to settle our differences.

Philip F. Lawler, president of the American Catholic Conference, has said:

> Our Lord Jesus Christ is the Prince of Peace, but that peace is not of this world—not a matter of simply stopping the armed conflicts among nations. Conflicts will continue, and armaments will threaten, until all nations are reconciled in Christ. And since the causes of war are always found in the hearts of men, the Christian's final resource of peace lies in the power of prayer, not politics . . . . A nation's defensive capacity can make war less likely, or less horrible. But no earthly defense can make war impossible, because no earthly defense can resolve the conflicts among men. There is no political formula that can ensure peace . . . . So in the battle for peace, we as Christians should rely most heavily on our one unanswerable weapon: prayer.[2]

As evangelical Christians let us reaffirm our belief in the sovereignty of God, the return of Christ and personal resurrection. This world is indeed coming to an end. The central point in Scripture is that judgment belongs to God. Do we not alter the meaning of the word *maranatha* to equate it with the coming of a man-made nuclear holocaust?

As Christians, we look to the future with confidence

because we believe in divine Providence. Harold O.J. Brown has written, "It is surely true that the proliferation of nuclear weapons increases the chance that someday they will be used again much more devastatingly than at Hiroshima and Nagasaki. But we must also recognize that this eventuality cannot happen except in the context of God's plan for the ages and with His permission."[3]

Does this mean the risks of nuclear war appear less awful and ultimate to Christians? Yes. That must be said or we deny what we claim about Easter. Does this mean we are less concerned about nuclear war? No. The crucial difference is that our concern is motivated not by fear (although, faithless servants that we are, there is fear) but by stewardship of God's creation.

All rational persons are concerned about the survival of the race. The ultimate folly would be to trivialize this. These are critical times and there is a distinct possibility that life on this planet could be reduced immeasurably.

However, in saying that it is worth any price to prevent nuclear conflicts, the premise is that morally and politically, nothing matters—nothing, that is, except survival. This attitude will make survival less likely. When survival becomes the highest ethic, we are in trouble. If there is nothing worth dying for, there is nothing worth living for.

Dr. James Schall of Georgetown University has said,

The continued life of "man" on earth—an abstraction down the ages—seems perilously near to substituting itself for the classical teachings about immortality and personal resurrection. From this arises a theoretical method to reabsorb the individual into the collectivity. Further, the principle of survival at any cost, of security as such, seems one of the main justifications for a sort of voluntary entrance into actual tyranny in which nothing is worth opposition except physical death, particularly death of the species.[4]

For some, the *new immortality* is the survival of the race. As Evangelicals, we believe in personal resurrection.

What kind of peace are we seeking? The peace called for by some seems to be nothing more than the absence of war. But true peace is the result of justice. It is not the absence of something, but fullness of right order. Peace without justice is the continuation of moral violence by other means. Solzhenitsyn says, "The movement 'against war' falls far short of filling the demands of a movement 'for peace' because of its acquiescence in the continuation of moral violence. Worse, such movements corrupt the word peace by applying it to this capitulation."

What kind of peace are we seeking? Robert Reilly has written:

> In his first speech before the AFL-CIO on June 30, 1975, Solzhenitsyn gave as an example of moral myopia the headline run in a major newspaper after the U.S. defeat in Southeast Asia. It read "The Blessed Silence." "This is celebrating the silence of the grave. Do the screams of butchered Cambodians make a sound if they are not heard in the West? Apparently not; all is quiet, all is blessed peace. More people have been killed in Southeast Asia since the withdrawal of the United States than during the entire war. Peace be with you? This is the peace brought to Southeast Asia in part by the anti-war movement, a peace worse than war.

"There were no boat people fleeing Viet Nam during the worst of the war; they only fled the peace. Peace be unto you? The incense celebrating this blessed peace is the multi-colored cloud of yellow rain that descends upon Hmong villagers who die from vomiting their own blood. This benediction is now being bestowed upon Afghanistan. This kiss of peace is poisoned."[5]

Among those who are witnesses for peace are the "Peace Churches." They have made a positive witness and pricked our consciences. These dedicated and sincere congregations have been islands of conviction in a world of pragmatism. Historically these churches have been separatists. They have not had the responsibility for government and diplomacy. Yet contemporary pacifism has never resolved the problem that plagued its forebearers: How should the pacifist conviction be related to the business of government? George Weigel has written:

Some pacifist churches and organizations have been heavily influenced by New Left teachings about the guilt of America and the promise of communism to the point where ethical selectivity has become a major problem. They condemn one side's participation in the arms race, but not the other's; they focus human rights' attacks on some kinds of government (usually authoritarian right) and not others; they reject personal participation in American military services while tacitly endorsing revolutionary violence by Third World forces deemed ideologically acceptable.[6]

In the mainstream of Christianity, pacifism has never been a prevailing view. Augustine wrote in his sermon on the healing of the centurion's son: "If Christian teaching forbade war altogether, those looking for the salutary advice of the gospel would have been told to get rid of their arms and give up soldiering. But instead they were told, 'rob no one by violence or by false accusation, and be content with your wages' (Luke 3:14). If the gospel ordered them to be satisfied with their pay, then it did not forbid a military career."

Many of the Christians in the primitive church refused to serve in the army because Roman military service involved a confession of the emperor's godhood that was clearly incompatible with Christianity. The military ceremonies of the Roman Empire were full of what the early church considered to be pagan rituals. There participation in military service was idolatrous.

None of the great reformers of the Church have been pacifists. Consider Luther, Calvin, Knox, and Wesley. All recognized the necessity of military defense in a fallen world.

Dr. Francis Schaeffer has written, "What should be our biblical perspectives on military preparedness? I would say that from my study of Scriptures, it is nothing less than lack of Christian love to not do what can be done for those gripped in the power of those who automatically and logically oppress. *This is why I am not a pacifist.* I am not a pacifist because pacifism in this fallen world in which we live means that we desert the people who need our greatest help."[7]

In our pursuit of peace we must avoid emotional sentimentality and think clearly. The German sociologist Max Weber draws a distinction between the *Ethics of Intention* and the *Ethics of Responsibility.* An "ethics of consequences" must take precedence over an "ethics of intentions." It would be well to remember that no democracy has ever gone to war because it was strong. In fact, a good argument could be made that military weakness invites war. Remember Munich! Winston S. Churchill, III, has said, "The peace activist of the 1930's led us directly into the Second World War by causing the Western democracies to disarm in the face of the growing Nazi build-up. To disarm today in the face of the growing Soviet build-up would be catastrophic."[8]

Hitler attacked Poland because France and Great Britain were unprepared and he misread them concerning their will to fight. The Japanese attacked Pearl Harbor because we were unprepared and they did not think we had the will to defend ourselves. Argentina attacked the Faulklands because they did not think Great Britain had the will or ability to fight.

It would be tragic if the Soviet Union were to misread America. We must never leave them in any doubt as to the strength of the Western alliance and our determination to ensure the survival of freedom and democracy.

Dr. Schaeffer said:

> Winston Churchill said immediately after the war that with the overwhelming forces of the Soviets they could easily dominate Western Europe to the Atlantic Ocean if it were not for the fact of being deterred by the United States having the atomic weapons . . . Europe would even more today than in Winston Churchill's day be subject to either military or political domination of the Soviets if it were not for the atomic weapon . . . . If the balance is now destroyed, there is no doubt in my mind that either militarily or politically the greatly superior Soviet Forces in Europe would soon overshadow Western Europe . . . .

Unilateral disarmament in this fallen world, and with the Soviets' materialistic, anti-God base, would be totally utopian and romantic and lead, as utopianisms always do in a fallen world, to disaster. Further, it may sound reasonable to talk of a freeze at the present level or "we won't ever use atomic weapons first"; but thinking it through, either of these equals practical unilateral disarmament. The atomic deterrent is removed and Europe stands at the absolute mercy of the overwhelmingly superior Soviet forces.

I am convinced that if the Bible-believing people now go along with the concept of "peace in our time" under the plausible concern and fear of atomic warfare (which we all certainly feel), our children and grandchildren will curse us quite properly for not doing something at this moment to restrain the drift toward the loss of Western Europe and other places to Soviet expansion . . . .

Those who say they are not for unilateral disarmament, but whose position equals unilateral disarmament, are those who, like Chamberlain, will bring war.[9]

I have yet to meet anybody who would dispute what we all know about the horror of nuclear war. It must be the prime objective of all of us to do all we can, as churches and as individuals, to see that we never have a world war in the nuclear age. But I believe it is vital that we should be ruled in these matters by reason and not by our emotions. Yes, we have peace as our objective. But let us seek it through strength, and let us not have as our aim unilateral disarmament, which could be catastrophic.

Another question we must honestly face is, would nuclear disarmament make a conventional war more likely? What are the practical consequences of various arms-control suggestions? Would a decrease in nuclear weapons lead to an increase in conventional armament? If we make nuclear war less likely, do we simultaneously make conventional war more likely, or even more deadly? There were over fifty million persons killed in World War II. With improved technology, think of the possibilities of a conventional war today! Our goal must not just be to end nuclear war. We must work to eliminate all forms of war as a means of settling disputes.

There are many who are questioning the morality of deterrence. But I would insist that arms control efforts, in order to be a morally superior alternative to nuclear deterrence, *must be able to produce peace, the security of states, and the freedom of peoples.* A case can be made that rationally-operated deterrence is morally preferable to either war or the surrender of our most cherished political values: values that are themselves based on Judeo-Christian moral claims about the sanctity of individual human beings. Here again, an "ethics of consequences" must take precedence over an "ethics of intentions."

No morally sensitive person can fail to feel the ethical dilemma of nuclear deterrence. It is not the system that we would deliberately choose; but it is the system we have created because, given the alternatives, it seemed at each point in its evaluation to be the lesser of two evils.

The deterrence system that has maintained nuclear peace between the super powers for thirty-eight years has developed in order to avoid the morally repugnant choice of nuclear war or surrender to totalitarianism. The merit of nuclear weapons lies in their ability to ensure that they will never be used.

Pope John Paul II said in his message to the United

Nations Special Session on disarmament, "In current conditions, deterrence based on balance, certainly not as an end in itself but as a step on the way towards a progressive disarmament, may still be judged morally acceptable."

May I remind you there is one condition even worse than a balance of terror, and that is an imbalance of terror. Richard Neuhaus has written:

> Whatever one thinks about the differences between nuclear and other weapons, the question finally arises how most effectively to reduce the risk of their being used.
>
> Not everyone agrees, however, that effectiveness is the main question. There is a strong school of thought that the issue is of making a clear moral witness . . . . Such an approach would seem to divorce moral witness from political judgment. The debate over the pacifist alternative must confront the question of violence in history. In our age it must encompass not only "conventional" warfare but biological, chemical, laser, and other instruments of violence which would not be attended by a ban on nuclear weapons. At its heart is whether we are responsible before God for the probable consequences of the positions we take, or whether we are simply to say NO to war and YES to peace, and leave whatever may be the policy implication and their consequences up to God. Are those who take the latter position "fools for Christ," or, as Reinhold Niebuhr would have it, "just plain fools"?[10]

I am convinced that military balance is essential to peace in the kind of world in which we live. But how are we to end this madness?

Arms control is, of course, a first step. It is necessary because the extreme military expenditures are not only causing great sacrifices to the peoples of the world, but the specter of global destruction is sobering to all responsible people.

We want not only arms control—we must insist on arms reduction. This is most likely to be achieved if we bargain from strength rather than from weakness. We reduced our military forces unilaterally during the seventies. The Soviets did not reciprocate. Why do we think they would now?

Since 1968, the United States has not deployed a single strategic nuclear missile. We have been absolutely constant at 1,710 submarine and silo-launch missiles. Has that been reciprocated by the Soviets? Not a bit. The Soviets during the same fifteen-year period have been adding two nuclear missile launchers every week—one hundred per year—until they have managed to shift the balance of power, once massively in favor of NATO and the West, to the point where it stands today, heavily in favor of the Soviet Union.

After we have considered all the political and military solutions to peace and disarmament we all need again to be reminded that this is essentially a spiritual question. "For we are not contending against flesh and blood, but against the principalities, against the powers, against the world rulers of this present darkness, against the spiritual hosts of wickedness in the heavenly places" (Eph. 6:12).

As evangelical Christians let us not be duped into secular answers and fail to recognize the nature of our adversary. This is a struggle of ideas and ideals! This is essentially a spiritual struggle! Are we suffering from spiritual exhaustion in the West, as Aleksandr Solzhenitsyn has suggested?

Does not the urgency of the hour call for a spiritual awakening as much as anything else? If America falls it may not be because of marching armies from without, but from moral corruption from within. May America regain a sense of "national purpose." May faith in God with peace, justice and freedom for all inspire us. As evangelical Christians may we recommit our lives to Jesus Christ with all that this implies.

When people do not understand the purpose for which they live, they find it difficult to exert the effort necessary to keep alive. Our chief purpose is "to glorify God and enjoy Him forever." And we look to that day "when the kingdom of the world has become the kingdom of our Lord and of his Christ . . . the wolf and the lamb shall feed together . . . nations shall not . . . learn war any more" (Rev. 11:15; Isa. 65:25; 2:4).

Notes

1. Robert Jastrow, *Commentary*, March, 1983, p. 30.
2. Philip F. Lawler, *Justice and War in the Nuclear Age* (Washington D.C.: University Press of America, 1983), pp. 1-4.
3. Harold O.J. Brown, *United Evangelical Action*, March-April, 1983, p. 8.
4. James Schall, "Intellectual Origins of the Peace Movement," in P. Lawler, *Justice and War,* p. 33.
5. Robert Reilly, "The Nature of Today's Conflict," in P. Lawler, *Justice and War,* p. 6.
6. George Weigel, *Peace and Freedom* (Washington, D.C.: Institute on Religion and Democracy, 1983), pp. 36-37.
7. These remarks were taken from Schaeffer's speech "The Secular Humanist World View versus the Christian World View and Biblical Perspectives on Military Preparedness" given at the Mayflower Hotel in Washington, D.C., on June 22, 1982.
8. Francis Schaeffer, *Imprimis*, December, 1982, p. 1.
9. Schaeffer's speech of June 22, 1982, as cited.
10. Richard Neuhaus, "Consider the Ethics of Consequences," *Eternity*, October, 1982, p. 28.

Chapter Thirteen

America's Strength Is the Best Guarantee of World Peace

by David Breese

In this present hour, 25 percent of the world is at war. We hear the disquieting report that in 1982 fifty thousand soldiers have died on the battlefields of earth. No one can view with anything but profound sorrow the abrasions between nations and peoples in our time and profoundly wish that a day of peace might come to this troubled world of ours.

In such an age, we listen with new attention to the words of Christ in the Sermon on the Mount as He said, "Blessed are the peacemakers, for they shall be called the children of God" (Matt. 5:9). Peacemaking, commended by the Saviour, is significantly a part of the ministry to which all believers have been called.

Thinking about this call, we are instantly struck with the fact that we have a most complex problem before us.

That complexity appears to be made even more complicated by the exigencies of our convoluted era. The call to
peacemaking means little without first knowing of what
war we are speaking. Surely the present conflicts, in a
very basic sense, include two wars.

The war between fallen man and the eternal God.
Humanity is even now at war with heaven. The rulers of
earth take counsel together against the Lord and against
His anointed saying, "Let us burst their bonds asunder,
and cast their cords from us" (Ps. 2:3). They imagine in
their vanity that they can win in a war against God. As a
result of this corporate and individual rebellion against the
Lord, each human being on earth is even now a child of
wrath (Eph. 2:3) and is, as a consequence, under divine
condemnation. The world, then, is already under judgment because it has not believed in the name of the only
begotten Son of God.

No discussion therefore of human peace can be related
to reality if it does not take into account man's lack of
peace with God. Most do not take this towering fact into
account and therefore most discussions concerning peace
are merely empty, verbal exercises.

The war between man and himself. The human soul, at
war with itself, knows not of "the peace of God, which
passes all understanding" (Phil. 4:7). For all men "the conflict within myself," while unresolved, makes the external
world a place of similarly unresolvable conflicts. What
rationality, what peace can be found in a global society pop-
ulated by individuals who are a habitation of warring drag-
ons?

All calls for orderly social activity assume individual
rationality and moral responsibility as a constraint to violence in the external society. These necessary prerequi-
sites, apart from "the peace of God which passes all
understanding" will be assumed as present only by the

wishful and the deluded.

Peacemaking then must first and always take the form of a call to the lost to accept the gift of peace which God has made available only through the finished work of Christ on Calvary's cross. "There is no peace, says my God, for the wicked" (Isa. 57:21).

The call to peace must then take the form of the call to spiritual maturity on the part of all who believe. The implanted Word in the believing heart will produce "the peace of God," the imperative base of any social peace which God may give.

PEACE IN SOCIETY

Of interest to us all is now the question of producing some form of social peace, peace on earth or a measure thereof. What course shall we advocate as to national policy, corporate Christian activity and personal endeavor to produce this result?

To answer this question, we must first ask what disturbs social peace? What or who is causing the wars and the threats thereof? No *effect* can be altered apart from addressing and if possible altering the *cause* or *causes* of that effect. Why, from whence, are our present conflicts? The provenience of the abrasions of our present world are several:

The Soviet-Communist intention of world conquest. The towering political reality of our time is the fact that a militant, atheistic ideology has captured a major segment of our world and is now mobilizing that segment toward the conquest of the earth. The Communist intention to conquer the world is its avowed, openly stated public policy. This policy has been repeated regularly in its publications so that the Communist design toward world conquest is a fact known to all. Dozens of formerly free nations of the earth, if they could, would tearfully testify that the Communists' boast of world conquest is no empty threat. So, Abba Eban said, "The real disturbers of the peace of the world are the Soviet Communists."

The Arab anti-Israel attitude. Most of the nations of the Arab world are in a continued state of war against the nation of Israel. Not only do they refuse to recognize the existence of a state called Israel but are on public record as intending, if they can, to push Israel into the sea. The consequence is that the Israelis have fought five wars in the Middle East in their battle for survival. Even now another war with the Syrians, backed by the Soviet Union, is publicly threatened. Mid-East conflict, potentially nuclear in nature, could draw in the big powers of the world. All agree that it is a potential flashpoint for a global war.

The resurgence of Islamic fundamentalism. The escalation to power of the Shiite Islamic sect has brought to the Moslem world a new, potentially deadly volatility. One consequence is that the largest battle since World War II was fought this last summer between Iran and Iraq. An Iraqi defeat could bring new power to Iran and prestige to Islamic fundamentalism across the entire Arab world. Iran then promises to march on Israel.

OPEC oil price pressure. The price of world oil was escalated by the OPEC nations to $34 a barrel. The consequence was that the OPEC nations were taking in at least 215 billion dollars a year with little possibility of investing such sums in their homelands. OPEC money therefore, particularly from the Saudi's, made it possible for the Palestine Liberation Organization to receive one million dollars a day to carry on its terrorist activities. Furthermore, OPEC money manipulation has unstabilized the economies of many nations of the West, bringing them to the point of economic desperation. Such desperation has more than often been one of the preludes to military conflict.

Liberation theology. A significant fact of our time is that a major segment of "organized Christendom" has been infected by the Marxist call to revolution. Using Christian words and misappropriating the call of Christ, liberation theology has captured perhaps one-half of the world of Catholicism, the Protestant left, and even the evangelical left. Liberation theology is, in fact, the spiritual subversion of the Church and the despicable call for that Church to involve itself in militant revolution. One writer calls it "the most serious problem which the Church has faced in all of its history."

Infantile, volatile political leadership. The presence of such people in positions of influence in public life as the Ayatollah Khomeini, Yasser Arafat, Colonel Khadafy has no small unstabilizing effect among the nations of earth. These leaders and many others are willing to hurl their puppet armies into bloody conflict for reasons which, in the West, would be called childish megalomania. No one can be sure of the future of Africa where the leader of Libya wants to be the new Caesar. Khomeini continues to unstabilize the entire Middle East while Arafat announces "another war against Israel is now necessary." These leaders, who live their lives beyond the pale of reason, make the world a dangerous place indeed.

Let us note that these sources of disturbance to world peace have nothing to do with American nuclear or military capability. Indeed, the fact is that these threatened forms of aggression are kept in check by American arms, especially its nuclear arms. The complexity of the situation called "world peace" in our present time certainly militates against simple answers which have merely to do with hardware and armies.

COURSE OF ACTION

In the midst of this complicated world scene, however, there is the towering, menacing shadow of the nuclear

arsenals of the nations, two superpowers and at least four
other not inconsiderable national nuclear forces. The
nuclear threat therefore looms in the minds of many as the
critical danger to mankind which is faced by our generation. Nuclear arms are now presented as being so vast in
their destructive capabilities that they demand new moral
considerations on the part of all. Therefore advocates of
peacemaking are now pressing a number of courses of
action to assure safety among the nations. They include:

A bilateral verifiable nuclear freeze

This position, along with its modifiers, has a superficial
appeal. "Wouldn't it be wonderful if we could call a halt to
the arms race and then give the nations time to think about
a course of action and the pursuit of world peace?" is the
argument. The problems, however, are many.

It cannot in fact be verified. It is true that we have
remarkable satellite surveillance but we cannot know what
goes on inside of this building or that. "On-site inspection"
is suggested as the answer but, of course, only the enemy
knows how many sites there are. One who bets his life on
such a program, and we do, needs some loving and understanding counsel.

It cannot be enforced. Suppose we did discover that the
Soviets were cheating? By that time, having frozen our
missile development like we did with our Minuteman program, we would have lost the ability to respond convinc-
ingly. A freeze program has many other liabilities.

It assumes "good faith" on the part of the Soviet Union.

*Even if it became a fact, it would put the U.S. at a grave
military disadvantage.*

*It presses upon us infinitely complicated, indeed impos-
sible, negotiations.*

*It ignores other nuclear nations—Britain, France,
Canada, India, others?*

Unilateral reduction by the United States
This suggested course of action appears to have most serious liabilities.

It assumes that the Soviets would follow our example. This bloc, which has now captured and enslaved many nations of the world, would be expected to reduce its military capability only by those who live in a world of unreality.

It really assumes that nuclear weapons are intrinsically immoral. This assumption is a giant step in philosophic thinking which attempts to prove that there is a point where quantity turns to quality. While attempting this proof, we must remember that conventional weapons have killed far more than have nuclear weapons. The Dresden firestorm with its 250 thousand fatalities gives abundant testimony to the difficulty of the qualitative nuclear argument.

Reference is now being made in the current discussions to Augustine and the Just War principles which he advocated. While the moral quality of all of our activities must never be forgotten, the Just-War ideas are largely an *ex post facto* set of considerations. Wars are rarely dissected by advance examination as to their moral quality. In advance of a war, no one knows what will be the extent of the battles and even if, in fact, a war will take place at all. To analyze a "potential future war" under a set of Just-War ideas will be found therefore to be difficult indeed.

CONSIDERATIONS
When considering, then, a course of action which must be advocated at this present time, we do well to keep in mind a number of considerations.

First, nuclear weapons are no threat to world peace when they are in the hands of the United States. Both history and our present policy testify that the U.S. has no intention towards world conquest and therefore denies any plan whatsoever to use its nuclear capability except for the defense of the United States homeland and Western civilization. A reduction therefore of America's nuclear capability would not *reduce,* rather it would *expand* the threat of global war.

Second, nuclear weapons in the hands of the United States, as against threatening world peace, have in fact tended to keep the peace. Their use on two occasions against the cities of Japan ended World War II. Their presence in the days of the Cuban crisis defused a threat to this hemisphere. The nuclear umbrella which America lifts over the free world is surely the human guarantor of the peace of Europe, the survival of Israel and the stabilizing of other areas of the world. It can reasonably be argued that American nuclear capability has prevented many smaller wars from becoming larger and more dangerous ones.

The testimony of history and our present experience therefore appears to dictate the wisdom of the policy of peace through strength. Given the predatory nature of our global enemies, the volatility of many areas of the earth where military confrontation now takes place, and many other considerations, the policy of peace through strength—nuclear strength on the part of the United States—appears to be dictated by the logic of our circumstances. To ignore the advance of a ravenous beast or to retreat in the face of an undefeated army is a dangerous activity indeed, practiced only by those for whom life is to be held in a low regard. In exactly this fashion, the military strength of the United States is the shield which protects the lives of billions of people and is one of the major guarantors for the continuance of Christian civilization.

We have then, in the American nuclear capacity, a deterrent to war. So much of the talk in our time appears to resent this function of nuclear weapons, that even when unused, they are threatening. Michael Novak has criticized this view by arguing:

> Those who intend to prevent the use of nuclear weapons by maintaining a system of deterrence in readiness for use do *intend* to use such weapons, but only in order *not* to use them, and do *threaten* to use them, but only in order to deter their use. That this is not mere rationalization is shown by the fact that several generations of nuclear weapons systems have become obsolete and been retired, without even having been used. These are considered the successful and moral systems.[1]

Let us pray that the nuclear force of Christian civilization will be successful in exactly this fashion.

Let us pray for something else. Above all else, let us pray that across our world will come not the immobilizing emotion of fear but the mighty impact of spiritual revival. The Church of our time needs the new knowledge of our impotence—our total incapacity apart from the help of our Sovereign Lord. In the last analysis, civilizations continue, not because of military, economic or political things, but because of spiritual things. Christians may differ as to the human course of action which we advocate, but we must not differ in our towering confidence that Jesus Christ is Lord. May the Lord of history move above and beyond our inarticulate discussions and fceble actions and continue to give to this generation the gift of peace and spiritual opportunity.

Note
1. Michael Novak, *Moral Clarity in the Nuclear Age* (Nashville: Thomas Nelson Inc., 1983). p. 59.

PART III

Where Is the Common Ground?

Old Testament Lesson:

May the Lord answer you when you are in distress;
    may the name of the God of Jacob protect you.
May he send you help from the sanctuary and grant
    you support from Zion.
May he remember all your sacrifices and accept your
    burnt offerings.
May he give you the desire of your heart and make
    all your plans succeed.
We will shout for joy when you are victorious and
    will lift up our banners in the name of our God.
May the Lord grant all your requests.

Now I know that the Lord saves his anointed;
    he answers him from his holy heaven with the
    saving power of his right hand.
Some trust in chariots and some in horses,
    but we trust in the name of the Lord our God.
They are brought to their knees and fall,
    but we rise up and stand firm.
O Lord, save the king! Answer us when we call! (Ps. 20,
NIV).

Rejoice greatly, O Daughter of Zion!
    Shout, daughter of Jerusalem!
See, your king comes to you, righteous and having
    salvation, gentle and riding on a donkey,
    on a colt, the foal of a donkey.
I will take away the chariots from Ephraim and
    the war-horses from Jerusalem, and the
    battle bow will be broken.
He will proclaim peace to the nations.
His rule will extend from sea to sea and from
    the River to the ends of the earth (Zech. 9:9,10, *NIV*)

New Testament Lesson:
Peace I leave with you; my peace I give you.
I do not give to you as the world gives. Do not
let your hearts be troubled and do not be afraid (John
14:27, *NIV*).

May the God of peace, who through the blood of the eternal covenant brought back from the dead our
Lord Jesus, that great Shepherd of the sheep, equip
you with everything good for doing his will, and may
he work in us what is pleasing to him, through Jesus
Christ, to whom be glory for ever and ever. Amen (Heb.
13:20,21, *NIV*).

Chapter Fourteen

Can Christians Work Together for Peace?

by John A. Bernbaum

What insights can Christians gain from Scripture when it comes to understanding and responding to the threat posed by nuclear weapons? What conclusions can be reached when followers of Jesus Christ, who are "transformed by the renewal" of their minds (Rom. 12:2), think about the nuclear arms race? These are the questions which we must now face after reflecting on the preceding chapters of this book.

Can Christians offer a message of hope in light of all the alarming cries of despair that can be heard today? In a world where the two superpowers collectively possess over fifty thousand nuclear warheads, with a destructive power of 1.5 million times that of the Hiroshima bomb, and plan to build thousands more, are there any answers or reasons for hope? "The best and the brightest" of our national leaders and opinion-makers exhaust the limits of their knowledge very quickly. When faced with the terrible prospect of nuclear holocaust, the only answers they can give us are: "We need more education," "We must be reasonable and use human ingenuity to work things out," or "We must overcome our ignorance or deliberate neglect of the nuclear problem and, for the sake of mankind, abolish all nuclear weapons for reasons of self-survival." Education, reason and fear of self-destruction—hardly answers that bring much comfort in the present crisis.

Can evangelical Christians offer anything better? Do we have anything else to say? The contributors to this volume have struggled with that very issue, although they have approached this question from many different perspectives and denominational backgrounds. As evangelical Christians, these authors shared a significant theological "common ground" which was largely assumed. This unstated unity of biblical truths, and Christ Himself, offer us hope because they give us a starting point for our dialogue.

The theological "common ground" that sets evangelicalism apart from the rest of the American religious community can be found in the "five fundamentals" of orthodox Protestant Christianity: (1) the infallible authority of Scripture, (2) the virgin birth of Christ, (3) His substitutionary atonement, (4) His bodily resurrection and anticipated second coming, (5) and His miracle-working power. It is on this ground that evangelicalism stands, and any possibility for unity in the Church, as a Body of Christ, requires agreement on these tenets of faith as a minimum.

These were the unstated areas of agreement, but what about the issue of war and peace in the nuclear age? How are we to understand our calling and task as peacemakers in a world of violence? Rather than highlighting the differences between the views of the contributors or engaging in a comparative analysis of pacifism versus Just-War theory versus deterrence, we must seek to identify where we as Christians have unity and where the light of Scripture leads us in our effort to be obedient to God's commands for right living in our present situation.

THE COMMON GROUND

Despite their differences, the contributors to this volume are in agreement on certain biblical truths which we can call "the common ground."

God desires peace for the world. The biblical concept of *shalom* is a magnificent picture of God's view of peace which involves wholeness, well-being, health, contentment, tranquility and sound relationships (Judg. 6:24; Ps. 147; Isa. 55:8-12; Jer. 29:11; 1 Cor. 14:33). The Hebrew understanding of *shalom* reflects the original state of affairs in the Garden of Eden (Gen. 1:29-31; 2:7,9) before sin entered the world. Biblical peace involves a "right relationship" with God the Creator, with ourselves, with our neighbors, and with nature—a fourfold vision that no human-created ideology has ever matched! God's view of peace is radically different from the world's view (John 14:27). Peace is not just the absence of violence; it is not just a stable environment that allows people to be left alone to "do their own thing." God's peace, "which passes all understanding" (Phil. 4:7), is much richer, much more constructive in character.

The Bible clearly demonstrates that peace is a "gift of God" (Ps. 20; Isa. 26:12; John 14:27). Scripture repeatedly describes God as a "God of Peace" (Isa. 19:18-25; 1 Cor. 14:33; Heb. 13:20,21) and His Son, Jesus Christ, as the "Prince of Peace" (Isa. 9:6). The origin of peace is not to be found with humanity or as a logical result of human reasoning, but in the very character of the Triune God. God, not humanity He created, gives peace (Isa. 2:2-4;

11:1-9; Hos. 2:18; Zech. 9:9,10). Peace will come not as a result of humanity's efforts but by the gracious gift of the Creator as men and women choose righteous living in obedience to His commandments. There is a difficult tension in Scripture on this subject: God grants peace as He chooses and no "theology of works" will ever enable us to "earn" it, yet God instructs us that being in right relationship is best and will bring *shalom.*

Biblical peace is linked to justice and righteousness (Isa. 59:8; Jer. 6:14). Scripture repeatedly shows that peace, as a characteristic of God, is intimately related to justice and righteousness, which are also parts of God's character. To work for peace without seeking to overcome structures of injustice makes little sense in light of God's Word. There can be no "military solution" which brings the real peace of *shalom.* Peace will only result when people are in "right relationship"—or living justly—with each other. Again, unlike the world's view of peace, the biblical view is not just negative or individualized. Peace linked to justice involves wholeness, health, and tranquility for a community of people.

Sin and evil break relationships and cause violence to occur. Scripture gives us a clear picture of the radical nature of evil (Gen. 3; Deut. 30:15-20; Zech. 7:8-14; Rom. 7:7-25). Although God is the Lord of history, Satan craftily seeks to oppose and frustrate God's rule. The Apostle Paul warns us that the real struggle in history is on a spiritual plane and that demonic forces are evident in historical events bringing violence, destruction, and death (Eph. 6:10-18; 2 Thess. 2:7-12). Just as biblical peace is more than the absence of violence, so evil—according to the Word of God—is not merely the absence of the good; evil is a terrible enemy of humanity and the source of human misery. Men and women can never overcome evil, manifested in individuals or in corporate structures, by their own power. Only God can overcome evil (Ps. 37; Amos 5) and He enables us to resist it (Jas. 4:7,8). We need to be realistic in our understanding of evil and place our hope not in human ingenuity or human reason but in the victory of the cross of Jesus Christ. The power of Satan has been broken and, although he still is the source of violence and suffering in the world, we know that God can and will subdue evil and bring judgment on the wicked.

The Holy Spirit is the Enabler who helps Christians in their pursuit of peace. Despite sin and its resulting violence in the world, we have been empowered by our Sovereign God. Once again, in contrast to the world's view that mankind must work for peace with its utmost energies out of a sense of fear or out of a desire for survival, the Bible encourages Christians by telling us that the Spirit of God will strengthen us and give us the ability to do infinitely more than we could ever do on our own strength (Eph. 3:20). In fact, God tells us a remarkable truth: in our weakness and dependency on Him we will find strength (2 Cor. 12:9,10)!

The beginning point for any Christian peacemaker must be a "right relationship" with the Triune God (Rom. 5:1-11; Phil. 4:4-7). If we are not at peace with God ourselves, how can we truly be peacemakers? If we do not know the love of God for us and have not experienced His grace toward us despite our lack of merit, then we know very little about the true nature of peace. If, on the other hand, we have peace with God, then we have a glimpse of the kind of peace for which we should be working. It is deeply troubling to see Christians, claiming to be peacemakers, in conflict with other Christians and in fact unwilling to be identified with one another because they differ on the practical political solutions which, in their judgment, would lead to peace. A saving faith in Jesus Christ, which makes a person into a new creation (Eph. 4:22-24), is where a biblical peacemaker must be grounded.

Working for peace on a corporate level, between nations or among political groups or even in a family, *requires the practice of peacemaking on an individual level.* If we are not reconcilers and healers in our own personal relationships, how can we meaningfully work for peace on a grander scale? Scripture calls us to "seek peace, and pursue it" (Ps. 34:14), but how can we pursue what we have never experienced? When Isaiah tells us that separation from God results in our not knowing the "way of peace" (59:8), the opposite is also true! As we learn to live a life of love, according to the teachings and deeds of Jesus Christ (John 15:9-17), as we learn to offer ourselves as a servant to others as Christ did for us (Phil. 2:5-11), then—and only then—can we meaningfully work for peace on a national or international level.

As a biblical people, we need a vision for peace. We cannot work for peace in a practical way without a vision shaped by our hope for the future which Scripture beautifully provides. Hope, not fear, should motivate us. The Bible describes God's desire of *shalom* for the world, a *shalom* which has implications not only for our personal lives but also for how society itself should function. The graphic picture portrayed by Isaiah (chaps. 60–62) and Micah (4:1-5) or recorded in Revelation (chap. 21) is a divine norm which God has given us as our hope. While we will never experience this peace in its fullness until Christ returns in all His glory, we can understand our present reality in light of that promised future. Here is another one of those tensions in Scripture: the peace of the Kingdom of God, a Kingdom which is both a present reality *and* a future hope, will never be complete until Christ's second coming; yet our task is to live as peacemakers in our present situation with that vision of God's peace as a goal toward which we are working.

As a biblical people, we need a practical understanding of peace which we must apply to our present situation. We cannot honestly hold to a vision of peace if we do not try to apply that vision of peace in practical ways. We must be committed to work for peace, not just committed to a general vision which is solely future-oriented. Being committed to work for peace means beginning with prayer and meditation, not political action; but it also means engaging in political action, not just prayer and meditation. Peacemaking, as a part of our lives as followers of Christ, should be an active calling, not a passive posture (Matt. 5:9; Heb. 12:14). Scripture instructs us to resist evil and to overcome evil with good (Rom. 12:21); it also challenges us to seek the peace of the land (Jer. 29:4-9; Prov. 24:11,12). This is the "ministry of reconciliation" which the Apostle Paul wrote about in Ephesians (2:11-18).

IDENTIFYING THE OBSTACLES

With all this "common ground" given to us by Scripture, the evangelical community should be newly invigorated. What are the obstacles that have prevented us in the past from truly understanding and responding to this biblical concept of peace? Why have we been unable to grasp its fullness or to implement its substance?

While it will not be possible nor desirable to review the history of evangelicalism in America in this brief chapter, we can identify five principal obstacles which stand in the way: (1) our privatized Christian faith; (2) our dual world view; (3) our perception of world peace as a political rather than a spiritual issue; (4) our unwillingness to challenge our society's values and practices; (5) and our simplistic labeling of opposing views and our unwillingness to engage in open dialogue.

First of all, *American Evangelicals have embraced a privatized Christian faith.* We have emphasized the personal redemption given to us through the sacrificial death of Jesus Christ and have stressed the need to proclaim the good news of Christ's saving power. We have raised generations of children who have been taught that Christ is their personal Saviour and who have developed admirable devotional lives of daily Bible study and prayer. Unfortunately, however, for many of us our God remains a private God who is Lord of our personal lives, but not much more. We read Scripture through this same lens—and we focus on passages about personal redemption and holy living and ignore all the rest. This type of thinking also leads to a Christianity characterized by a "rugged individualism." What is lost is the corporate sense of the Church of Jesus Christ as a body that is dependent on the relationship between each of its diverse parts (Rom. 12:3-8; 1 Cor. 12:12-31).

This privatization leads us into a second, related problem, that of a dual world-view. Once we have isolated our faith into the private realm and view our relationship with Jesus as an intensely "personal matter," that leaves the rest of our life in a completely separate compartment. Few Evangelicals would freely admit this, but most of us act this way. We see little relationship between our faith in Jesus and the way we conduct politics or do business. We are at a loss to understand how our careers fit into our calling to be "in Christ." What does our faith have to do with filling out income tax forms, driving our automobile, working as a business leader with labor and management, or holding elected office?

Our social and political surroundings push us in that direction. A pillar of our constitutional structure in the United States is the doctrine of the separation of Church and state—which is often misinterpreted to mean that religion and politics must not be mixed. A current myth of our society is that politics is "neutral" or value-free. Our public educational system and nationwide television also communicate in terms that are devoid of any explicit religious content. This continually implies that religion is not a necessary part of "real life."

The problem we face is this: Jesus Christ must be Lord of everything or He is Lord of nothing! We cannot give Him part of our lives and be true disciples of His. This is what has happened to Evangelicals on the issue of peace. We have repeatedly emphasized the "peace of God" as a biblical concept relating to our personal relationship to God or to our being "at peace" with ourselves. Both of these dimensions of peace are described in Scripture. But why have Evangelicals neglected the other dimensions of biblical peace—peace with our neighbors or among nations and peace with our natural surroundings? Our vertical relationship with God is important and so is "inner peace." However, we must not stop here; God's desire for us is also to be peacemakers on a horizontal plane—with other peoples, races and nations—and in relationship to His created world as good stewards.

This privatization and the resulting dualism have created a third obstacle: *Evangelicals have traditionally considered the issue of international peace a "political issue," not a spiritual one.* The Pasadena conference, by its very existence, is a move in the direction of overcoming this obstacle. Every speaker at the conference and every contributor to this book participated because of a desire to see the evangelical community seriously address the issue of peace in the nuclear age. While there were clear differences in terms of what political solutions are considered best, all agreed that the peace issue is a legitimate concern which Christians must address. That we can no longer be silent on this subject was the clear challenge addressed to the evangelical community by the Pasadena conference speakers.

Another obstacle for Evangelicals is our comfortable place in American society. Unlike the 1920s and 1930s when we were a despised subculture, Evangelicals are now "in." Some presidential candidates openly profess being "born again," while others deliberately court the so-called "religious vote." It is hard for us to be prophetic when we are near to or in the courts of power. For many of us, our allegiance as American citizens dominates our sense of commitment to the Church of Jesus Christ, that transnational body which supersedes the boundaries of nation-states. This is symbolically demonstrated in the terrible irony of the largest Catholic church in Hiroshima serving as the target for the American pilots, who were also Catholics, when the dropped the bomb in August, 1945, thereby initiating the nuclear age. What a haunting reminder of how Christians have killed other Christians throughout history in the name of their nation or race or tribe.

When we think about issues of war and peace, we often argue for the need to be "realistic," which usually means defending the national self-interest of the United States. Instead, our first priority should be our brothers and sisters in Christ. It is with these people that we should be reconciled, regardless of language, color or nationality. The Church of Jesus Christ, because of its multi-national character, should by definition be an agent for world peace!

It may well be that peacemaking in the nuclear age will require us to challenge the present policies of our government and the Soviet Union. The question quickly becomes one of whether we should seek to be comfortable or obedient. Peacemaking, in a world of violence where sin reigns in the hearts of all people, will not be a popular pursuit. It has never made for "good politics."

Finally, for those Evangelicals who have thought seriously about our peacemaking task in the nuclear age, *there will have to be a deliberate effort to overcome the obstacles of labeling opposing views with simplistic phrases.* Slogans like "Christian pacifism," "Just-War" or "peace-through-strength" can become excuses for avoiding the real issue. Deep, honest dialogue among Christians with diverse perspectives must take place. We have much to learn from each other. As John Stott suggested, for example, Just-War advocates concentrate on the need to punish evil and tend to forget the other biblical injunction to "overcome evil with good"; "Christian pacifists," on the other hand, concentrate on the need to overcome evil with good and tend to forget that, according to Scripture, evil deserves to be punished.

Historically, Just-War advocates in the Reformed tradition have emphasized the biblical doctrine of creation and the so-called cultural mandate, but have sometimes failed to understand the full implications of the Fall and the impact of sin on contemporary institutions. On the other hand, "Christian pacifists," by stressing the nonviolence of Christ's life and teachings, have sometimes failed to understand the full power of Christ's redemption achieved by His death on the cross. "Peace-through-strength" advocates, while emphasizing the fallen nature of man because of sin, have sometimes failed to understand that biblical peace and justice are of more concern to God than simple political freedom or "religious liberty." Open discussion, surrounded by times of worship and prayer, is needed in the struggle for biblical peacemaking in the nuclear age. Each perspective offers a balance to the others and it may be that we will have to live in this tension for the foreseeable future. Dismissing advocates of other perspectives with quick labels has hurt the Christian community in its calling to be peacemakers.

Spiritual renewal of the church is critically needed to

overcome these obstacles, and signs indicate that this is happening. A renewed awareness of the full implications of the lordship of Jesus Christ is a decisive factor in this spiritual renewal. As Evangelicals gain a new appreciation for Christ's lordship, the old dividing walls between our private and public lives begin to disappear. We can no longer maintain a dual world view which compartmentalizes Jesus into a spiritual closet labeled "personal business." If He is our Lord as well as our Saviour, then no sphere of our lives is outside His authority. Every dimension of our living— our relationships with family and friends, our businesses, even our politics—must be impacted by our faith in Christ.

A revitalized understanding of the Kingdom of God will also help Evangelicals overcome these hindrances. When we consider that the Kingdom of God is both future hope *and* present reality, that it has both spiritual *and* physical dimensions to it, and that we are instructed by Jesus to pray for its coming "on earth as it is in heaven," the walls of our privatized faith are again under assault. One characteristic of God's Kingdom is His desire for *shalom*. As we study Scripture in order to understand this four-fold vision of biblical peace, we can no longer be satisfied with preaching or teaching that emphasizes only one or two dimensions of peace while avoiding others.

New emphasis on the costs of discipleship is also enabling the evangelical church to overcome its enculturation, its comfortable place in American society. Christ's teachings about suffering (Matt. 5:10; 16:24-27; John 15:18-25), a theme also repeatedly discussed by the Apostle Paul (Rom. 8:16,17; Phil. 1:29), remind us of the need to be obedient to God's Word regardless of the price.

The barriers are also breaking down between traditional perspectives on war and peace. The unique nature of nuclear weapons has forced most Christians to abandon the classical Just-War approach because the weapons by their very nature violate the traditional criteria cited in determining just use of force. This is evidenced by the fact that none of the contributors to this volume argued from a Just-War position. In fact, many of those who come from denominations that have held to that traditional perspective are now "nuclear pacifists." Old labels are not appropriate any more, which opens up the possibility for dialogue on a new basis.

The ultimate debate between Christians who are pacifists and those who are not will not be easily settled. However, if both groups realize that a life of complete nonviolence is not a possibility in our present situation—since all citizens pay at least some taxes which support our police forces, if not our military—and at the same time that God hates violence and murder because He is the God of peace, the tension between the two views becomes more tolerable. Perhaps like the tension between God's sovereignty and humanity's free will, the tension between these views concerning the use of force cannot be resolved. This tension may be what God desires the Church to live with.

Evangelicals must agree that all political responses to the need for peace are ambiguous, as David Hubbard has suggested, if we are to overcome these obstacles.

There is more than one Christian approach to the problems involved in the nuclear arms race. We must be willing to practice charity and patience with each other as we earnestly search for the best way to achieve world peace and to rid the world of the threat of a nuclear holocaust. We must be willing to maintain our unity in Christ while pursuing different political solutions to the threat of nuclear war. If we are unified, that in itself is a significant step toward peacemaking within our own community. It would be an impressive sign to the rest of the world that those of us who openly confess the name of the Prince of Peace are willing to be at peace with others in the Church despite our differences.

Our ultimate hope lies in our belief in the Sovereign God of the universe, the Alpha and the Omega, the all-powerful Creator God who, at the same time, calls each one of us by name. He is the God of peace who desires for us a peace that is beyond our imagination. He has sent us His own Son, who was announced as the "Prince of Peace," and the Holy Spirit who will empower us to achieve what we could never do on our own. It is in God alone that our hope rests.

PART IV
Guide to Resources
A Selected Bibliography on the Christian
Faith and Warfare in the Nuclear Age

I. Christian Views Concerning War and Peace
   A. General Surveys of Traditional Christian Views on
       War and Peace

Bainton, Roland. *Christian Attitudes Toward War
   and Peace: A Historical Survey and Critical Re-
   evaluation.* Nashville, TN: Abingdon Press,
   1960.
   This is one of the best historical studies available on different Christian attitudes toward war;
   it divides Christian attitudes into three catagor-
   ies—pacifism, Just War and the crusade.
Clouse, Robert G., ed. *War: Four Christian
   Views.* Downers Grove, IL: Inter-Varsity
   Press, 1981.
   Four well-known Christian writers present

their different views on the subject of war and offer criticisms of the perspectives of the other three. The four views offered are nonresistance (Herman A. Hoyt), Christian pacifism (Myron S. Augsburger), the Just War (Arthur F. Holmes), and the crusade or preventative war (Harold O.J. Brown).

Craigie, Peter C. *The Problem of War in the Old Testament.* Grand Rapids: Wm. B. Eerdmans Publishing Co., 1978.

An insightful study of the Old Testament representation of God as a Warrior, God's revelation of Himself in a book which preserves an extensive amount of war literature, and the conflicting ethics which seem to exist between the Old and New Testaments.

Eller, Vernard. *War and Peace from Genesis to Revelation.* Scottdale, PA: Herald Press, 1981.

An examination of the subject of war and peace which takes into account Old Testament military material, the meaning of Jesus with respect to violence and the significance of the book of Revelation. This study weaves together insights from biblical study, theology, and ethics.

Ellul, Jacques. *Violence: Reflections from a Christian Perspective.* New York: Seabury Press, Inc., 1969.

A penetrating analysis of violence enlightened by the truths in Scripture.

B. Christian Pacifist Tradition

Aukerman, Dale. *Darkening Valley: A Biblical Perspective on Nuclear War.* New York: Seabury Press, Inc., 1981.

Arguing that the present controversy over

nuclear weapons is a theological, more than a political, question, Aukerman examines Scripture on the subject of where to find security and what following Jesus means in the nuclear age.

Kraybill, Donald B. *Facing Nuclear War: A Plea for Christian Witness*. Scottdale, PA: Herald Press, 1982.

A wide-ranging discussion of the problems of the nuclear age, along with a reminder that, in God's eyes, human pretensions at absolute power are ludicrous.

Sider, Ronald J. *Christ and Violence*. Scottdale, PA: Herald Press, 1979.

A comprehensive discussion of the effects of nuclear war, Christian positions of Just War and nonviolence, ways to work for peace and non-military means of national defense.

Wallis, Jim. *The Call to Conversion: Recovering the Gospel for These Times*. New York. Harper and Row, 1981.

In analyzing the meaning of Christian conversion, Wallis discusses the threat of nuclear war and the Christian calling to be peacemakers.

Yoder, John H. *The Politics of Jesus*. Grand Rapids: Wm. B. Eerdmans Publishing Co., 1972.

Yoder develops "the politics of the cross" based on Jesus' life, which leads to a position of nonviolence and an attitude of "revolutionary subordination."

C. Just-War Tradition

Holmes, Arthur F. ed., *War and Christian Ethics*. Grand Rapids: Baker Book House, 1975.

A study of ancient, medieval and modern Christian writers and their criticisms of warfare in

their own times largely based on Just-War criteria.

O'Brien, William V. *The Conduct of Just and Limited War.* New York: Praeger Pubs., 1981.
A comprehensive treatment of the nature of
modern warfare by a leading Catholic scholar.

Ramsey, Paul. *War and the Christian Conscience.*
Durham, NC: Duke University Press, 1981.
A classic study of Just-War theories and the
nature of rational armament.

Tucker, Robert W. *The Just War, a Study in Contemporary American Doctrine.* Baltimore, MD:
Johns Hopkins University Press, 1960.
While not written from a Christian perspective,
this book is a profound study of the moral appli-
cations of employing force in the nuclear age.

D. Defense of Deterrence

Barrs, Jerram. *Who Are the Peacemakers? The
Christian Case for Nuclear Deterrence.* West-
chester, IL: Crossway Books, 1983.
Arguing that pacifism is utopian and leads to terrible injustice, Barrs offers his defense of military strength as the best deterrent to war in
light of biblical views of justice and mercy.

Novak, Michael. *Moral Clarity in the Nuclear Age.*
Nashville: Thomas Nelson Publishers, 1983.
Written as a response to the pastoral letter on
war and peace by the American Roman Catholic
Bishops, Novak, a noted Catholic scholar, discusses the arguments for and against nuclear
armament. He argues that "to abandon deterrence is to neglect the duty to defend the innocent . . . "

Weigel, George. *Peace and Freedom: Christian
Faith, Democracy and the Problem of War.*

Washington, D.C.: Institute on Religion and Democracy, 1983.

Weigel is concerned that the desire for peace may drive the churches to support positions that make war more likely, rather than less. He argues for remaining faithful to the Christian gospel and the American democratic experiment, while pursuing world peace.

II. *The Nature of Weapons and Warfare in the Nuclear Age*

  A. Survey of the History of the Nuclear Arms Race

Freedman, Lawrence. *The Evolution of Nuclear Strategy.* New York: St. Martin's Press, 1981.

A scholarly survey of the strategic debate in the postwar period over doctrines of massive retaliation, limited war, counterforce targeting, and assured destruction.

Ground Zero. *Nuclear War: What's in It for You?* New York: Pocket Books, 1982.

A popularly written book designed as a primer on how we got into the present nuclear crisis, how a nuclear war might start and how a nuclear war can be prevented.

Kaplan, Jerome H. *Security in the Nuclear Age: Developing U.S. Strategic Arms Policy.* Washington, D.C.: Brookings Institution, 1975.

Although somewhat outdated, this study is still one of the best surveys of U.S. defense policies and strategic doctrines in the nuclear period.

Mandelbaum, Michael. *The Nuclear Question: The United States and Nuclear Weapons, 1946-1976.* Cambridge, U.K.: Cambridge University Press, 1979.

This book is a set of reflections, rather than a basic history, on American thinking about the problem of nuclear weapons.

B. Analysis of Comparative U.S.–U.S.S.R. Weapons Systems

Department of Defense. *Annual Report—Fiscal Year 1985*. Washington, D.C.: DOD, January, 1984.

An annual statement by the secretary of defense explaining the Pentagon's view of our military posture worldwide and the budget priorities for the upcoming year. This report includes a discussion of American and Soviet military capabilities and changes in the strategic balance.

International Institute for Strategic Studies. *The Military Balance, 1984*. London, U.K.: IISS, 1984.

One of the best annual compilations of material on military forces and regional power.

Stockholm International Peace Research Institute. *SIPRI Yearbook 1984*. Cambridge, MA: MIT Press, 1984.

An annual report which presents data on the arms race and worldwide military expenditures, including information about comparative U.S.–U.S.S.R. military power.

C. Effects of Nuclear War

Katz, Arthur M. *Life after Nuclear War: The Economic and Social Impacts of Nuclear Attacks on the United States*. Cambridge, MA: Ballinger Publishing Co., 1981.

Katz projects the qualitative and quantitative effects of both limited and full-scale attacks on the entire fabric of society.

Physicians for Social Responsibility. *The Final Epidemic: The Medical Consequences of*

Nuclear Weapons and Nuclear War. Chicago: Educational Foundation for Nuclear Science, 1981.
An analysis of the medical effects of nuclear war by a team of doctors concerned with removing the nuclear threat.

Schell, Jonathan. *The Fate of the Earth.* New York: Alfred A. Knopf, Inc., 1982.
A vivid portrayal of the total impact of a major nuclear war on the planet's total ecological system.

U.S. Congress, Office of Technology Assessment. *The Effects of Nuclear War.* Washington, D.C.: U.S. Government Printing Office, May 1979.
At the request of the Senate Foreign Relations Committee, this study analyzed four different levels of nuclear warfare and their effects on both American and Soviet societies.

For an excellent guide to additional resources on this subject, including audiovisual aids, a listing of organizations working for peace, and a brief description of curriculum materials for local congregations, see *Nuclear Holocaust and Christian Hope* (Downers Grove, IL: Inter-Varsity Press, 1982), written by Ronald J. Sider and Richard Taylor, pp. 295-317.

For information concerning the purchase of cassette tapes from the Church and Peacemaking conference held in Pasadena, California in May 1983, contact:

The Christian College Coalition
235 Second Street, N.E.
Washington, D.C. 20002